Nant Gwrtheyrn, by Suzanne Greenslade

DISCOVERING WELSHNESS

edited and introduced by
Fiona Bowie and Oliver Davies

GOMER

First Impression—1992

© Fiona Bowie and Oliver Davies

ISBN 0 86383 722 0

All rights reserved. No part of this book may be reproduced, stored in a retrieval system, or transmitted in any form or by any means, electronic, electrostatic, magnetic tape, mechanical, photocopying, recording or otherwise, without permission in writing from the Publishers, Gomer Press, Llandysul, Dyfed, Wales.

This volume is published with the Support of the Welsh Arts Council

Printed by
Gomer Press, Llandysul, Dyfed

Er cof am
Eryl Oliver Davies
ac â mawr ddiolch i
Gwynfor Evans

ACKNOWLEDGEMENTS

Our thanks are due to the following authors and publishers for permission to reprint the following:

'Border' by Gillian Clarke from *Letting in the Rumour,* Carcanet.

'On Translating Welsh Poetry (Cywydd)' by Tony Conran from *Profiles,* edited by Glyn Jones and John Rowlands, Gomer.

'Why I Write in Welsh' by Bobi Jones, 'Nant Gwrtheyrn' by R.S. Thomas and 'In John Jones Country' by Meic Stephens were published in *Planet.*

'The Welsh Language' by Bobi Jones from *Bobi Jones: Selected Poems,* translated by Joseph Clancy, and 'Elegy for Mr Lewis (Welsh)' by Meic Stephens from *Green Horse,* were published by Christopher Davies.

'Why do I Publish in Welsh?' by Judith Maro originally appeared in the *Anglo-Welsh Review.*

The photographs by David Bailey were published by The Ffotogallery (David Bailey and Susan Beardmore) to accompany the exhibition, David Bailey: Part of the Valleys Project, 1985.

CONTENTS

		Page
Preface		x
List of illustrations		xiii
Introduction		xiv
A Hidden Culture	*Phyllis Kinney*	1
Coming Home	*Sylvia Prys Jones*	5
'The Outer Loss shall be the Inner Gain'	*A.M. Allchin*	12
The man who was frisked of his china rugby ball	*Jon Dressell*	20
'Saeson yw ei rieni, 'chi'n gweld . . .'	*John Geraint*	27
A Language to Live By	*John Gillibrand*	31
The Importance of Identity	*Patricia Elton Mayo*	34
Border	*Gillian Clarke*	39
'A Disservice to Welsh Scholarship'	*Pennar Davies*	40
In John Jones Country	*Meic Stephens*	44
Elegy for Mr Lewis (Welsh)	*Meic Stephens*	53
Open Secrets	*Emyr Humphreys*	54
Choosing Wales	*Raymond Garlick*	55
'Modd i Fyw'	*Carl Clowes*	59
Nant Gwrtheyrn	*R.S. Thomas*	70
'Here in England'	*Suzanne Greenslade*	71
Welsh Hills	*Oliver Davies*	74
Talley Abbey	*Oliver Davies*	77
Hobson's Choice	*Zonia Bowen*	79
In England isn't it?	*Leigh Verrill-Rhys*	85
Return of the Native	*Jeffrey Gainer*	88
'So what's all the fuss about . . .?'	*Lena Rhys*	95
Welsh Winds	*Ben Ridler*	99
Cynghanedd	*Pat Neill*	104
On Translating Welsh Poetry (Cywydd)	*Tony Conran*	110
Why I Write in Welsh	*Bobi Jones*	111
The Welsh Language	*Bobi Jones*	117
Foreigners	*John Barnie*	118
Rhiannon, Mabon and Me	*Noragh Jones*	121
A Christian Civilisation	*Daniel Mullins*	128
Images of Wales	*Fiona Bowie*	132
Adnabod, Hanfod, Cymreictod	*M.A.K. Duggan*	136

Why do I Publish in Welsh?	*Judith Maro*	148
Welshness	*George Askey*	151
'Welsh by Proxy'	*Neil Caldwell*	157
At Bala	*Joseph Clancy*	163
The Last Laugh	*Tony Bianchi*	164
Acquiring an Inheritance	*Greg Hill*	172

| Contributors | | 176 |

PREFACE

The nature of Welsh identity, the role of the Welsh language within Wales, and the relationship which exists (or does not exist) between these two phenomena, is a never-ending source of fascination and frustration for the incomer and native alike. The idea of collecting together a series of personal reflections on this theme arose out of our awareness that the Welsh language, although in some ways central to any definition of 'Welshness', means very different things to different people. The contributors to this volume have all learnt, or re-learnt, Welsh as teenagers or as adults, although not all of them live in Wales. What they have in common is a desire to communicate what they have discovered through the window of the Welsh language, and it is our hope that these short reflections on some aspects of 'Welshness' will encourage others to take that same step. At the very least, we trust that the contributions in this volume will succeed in conveying something of the respect and gratitude which so many learners of Welsh feel towards Welsh-speaking Wales, as well as portraying the variety and complexity of this portion of Welsh society.

The book has grown organically with most of the contributors we originally approached suggesting other names in turn. There are many thousands of Welsh learners in Wales, as well as in other parts of the world, and this collection represents only a fraction of those we could have asked. Although we have tried to achieve some balance between geographical areas and backgrounds, the collection remains, necessarily, somewhat arbitrary in its scope.

We would like to thank all those who have so kindly agreed to put their thoughts on paper, as well as the many people who have encouraged and supported this book with their suggestions and good wishes. No attempt has been made to force the contributions into a particular mould or to reconcile different points of view. To do so would, we believe, have been counterproductive. Welshness is not an object waiting to be discovered, but a way of being and of relating to others. It is a social construct in which each of us plays our own unique role, either as onlooker or as participant, or perhaps as both. Welsh-speaking Wales has a present and a future as well as a past, and it is up to each one of us to take our part in shaping that future, if we so wish, or as Gwyn Alf Williams so eloquently expressed it in his 1979 BBC Radio Wales Lecture:

There is no historical necessity for Wales; there is no historical necessity for a Welsh people or a Welsh nation. Wales will not exist unless the Welsh want it. It is not compulsory to want it. Plenty of people who are biologically Welsh choose not to be Welsh. That act of choice is beyond reason. One thing, however, is clear from our history. If we want Wales, we will have to make Wales.

Fiona Bowie and Oliver Davies
Capel Curig
January 1992

ILLUSTRATIONS

	Page
1. Nant Gwrtheyrn, by Suzanne Greenslade	Frontispiece
2. Chapel Interior, Tythegston near Porth-cawl, by Suzanne Greenslade	14
3. Porth Town Centre, Rhondda, by David Bailey	28
4. Capel-y-Ffin, by Suzanne Greenslade	38
5. Penrhiwceiber Workingmen's Institute, by David Bailey	48
6. Apêl Tŷ'r *Faner,* Ymddiriedolaeth Nant Gwrtheyrn, by Robin Llwyd ab Owain.	64
7. Dafydd ap Gwilym, Talyllychau, by Fiona Bowie	78
8. 'Rhaid i'r Iaith Fyw!' by Suzanne Greenslade	115
9. Margam Abbey, by Suzanne Greenslade	130
10. Princetown, Ogmore Valley, by David Bailey	154

INTRODUCTION

Wyn Griffiths, writing in 1950 (words which have lost none of their pertinence), stated that:

> To the ordinary Englishman, the greatest of all strangeness is a strange language in a familiar country . . . Where else in this Island would he find his own language taking second place in daily life? . . . Our traveller realises that . . . somewhere on this journey he has crossed an unnoticed frontier . . . In spite of outward similarities, in architecture and in landscape, in face and figure, he becomes aware of differences. That sense of remoteness persists, and indeed grows stronger with time. Closer acquaintance with these people, he finds, tends to stress the points of difference: what is common ground between him and them is quickly accepted and loses its interest.

But what are these mysterious 'differences' which are perceptible to the stranger but which are so hard to define? One way of answering this question is to see how the exploration of 'Welshness' has affected the experiences and perceptions of individuals. No two people start from the same point or reach the same conclusions, but the cumulative effect of their observations and reflections is to weave a tapestry of many colours out of which some identifiable patterns begin to emerge.

It is perhaps important to state at this point what we are *not* trying to do with this book. We are not saying that there is only one Wales or one way of being Welsh, and that this is through the Welsh language. Wales, like the other nations within the United Kingdom, is made up of people of different linguistic and ethnic backgrounds. This pluralism and diversity is a human resource which should be fostered and valued. The desire for uniformity, whether it be for an English-speaking 'Britishness' or an exclusively Welsh-speaking Welsh identity, is to mistake uniformity for unity or for security, and to squander the gifts which our very differences entail. Nevertheless, we do believe that languages are more than merely convenient codes for communication. Languages are transmitters of culture in its broadest and most vital sense. Welsh is the oldest spoken language in Britain with a rich and varied literature, oral as well as written. It is also a living language, spoken daily by nearly half a million people. And, as the Welsh adage has it: *Cenedl heb iaith, cenedl heb galon* ('A nation without a language is a nation without a heart').

Our motive in collecting together these varied accounts of 'Welshness', seen from the perspective of those who have learnt the Welsh language, is to explore the notion of Welshness itself. We have chosen as contributors individuals who have *acquired* a knowledge of Welsh, in the hope that from their experience of discovery a fresh and illuminating light will be cast on old questions. Of course we are aware that Welsh learners constitute a small minority and that there are many born within the United Kingdom who first discover that the language exists—sometimes to their horror!—when they move into a Welsh-speaking area. But the message of our contributors is that there is much to be gained from learning the language: a new sense of Welsh identity, a deeper understanding of the people and country of Wales with its traditions and history, the discovery of community, of the values of a small people, conscious of their heritage, their culture, their strength and their vulnerability in the face of powerful outside forces.

What then is the unique contribution of Wales and its language to the world of the 1990s? In the seeming anonymity of much modern life and the deadening influence of a generally bland Anglo-American culture, the Welsh-speaking world is small enough to provide a sense of belonging. Welshness is more than a language, it is an awareness of a particular past which affects the interpretation of the future. The Welsh learner often makes this history and destiny their own, becomes involved in Welsh social or cultural life, and contributes to Wales through politics, publishing or in personal commitments and interactions of many kinds.

Welshness, then, is much more than possession of a language. It is a sense of community, identity, a world of culture, poetry, and proximity to the past, all of which draw upon the language, even in those areas in which Welsh is no longer spoken. Wales as a place with a specific culture is unthinkable without the language, either as a past influence, an image of Wales against which to define one's own identity, or as a vehicle for the values and myths of the community. We hope that this glimpse into the life and experience of a wide range of people, all of whom have made that journey into the Welsh language and the world it creates and sustains, will give those who do not speak Welsh a deeper understanding of the 'Welsh way' and will encourage those with the opportunity to set forth along that road bravely and with a good heart.

A HIDDEN CULTURE
Phyllis Kinney

'Come with me,' said my Welsh husband-to-be, 'I've got something interesting to show you.' We were in the village of Maentwrog for the purpose of getting a special licence to be married. As an American who had been living in Wales only a few weeks, I thought it a romantic errand and expected that his promise of 'something interesting' would also be romantic, with a bearing on our forthcoming marriage. I was thus considerably astonished, not to say taken aback, to be led to the Maentwrog graveyard. 'There,' said my Romeo, proudly pointing out a dilapidated gravestone, 'that is the grave of Edmwnd Prys.'

At that point I first realised that this country of Wales, which I was adopting as my future home, had a hidden culture which would only be opened with the key of the Welsh language. Had I been marrying an Englishman who had taken me to see the grave of, say, Edmund Spenser I would at least have heard the name and been able to place him among the Tudor poets. But the Welsh language and its culture was a closed book to me, apart from a few songs which I was able to sing in Welsh, parrot-fashion, without really understanding the words. I knew that Welsh was the first language of my prospective husband and his family, but all the Welsh speakers that I met were bilingual so that there was never any *necessity* to learn Welsh in order to be understood. And nobody shamed me into it, either. In fact, it was the very warmheartedness of the Welsh themselves that made me feel welcome in Wales and shielded me from the realisation that there was a whole world of Welshness which was closed to me without the key of the language.

That was in the late 1940s and I lived only eighteen months in Wales before we moved to England and then to America. In those years English became established as our family language and it was not until we returned in 1960 that the question of learning to speak Welsh arose. For me the question seemed peripheral, on the same level as the French, German and Italian which I had had to learn when I was studying opera in New York. I was still cocooned by the willingness of the Welsh speakers I knew to make allowances for their friend's American wife. And when I first came to Wales, there were no classes in the Welsh language for adult learners—indeed, I was assured that Welsh was so difficult it had to be learned in childhood or not at all. But by the 1960s, partly perhaps as a by-product of the excitement of that tumultuous decade, but certainly as a result of the ominous decline in the percentage of Welsh speakers, Welsh-language classes began to attract more and more students. And I became one of them.

It certainly wasn't easy. In those early days there was less emphasis on speaking and more on grammar and literature. So I learned my rules of mutation and read *Y Cymro* and continued to speak English. This was the pattern for some time but almost without my realising it, I was acquiring vocabulary through my reading which extended by now to magazine articles, novels and some poetry. Gradually my comprehension of the spoken language improved. By now my husband had begun to speak Welsh to me and I heard it on television and radio. But most of the people who came to the house were Welsh speakers, and I was increasingly embarrassed that they either had to speak English when I was present or appear impolite. So began an odd period when I would ask our Welsh friends to speak Welsh with me but I would reply in English.

How long such an unsatisfactory arrangement would have gone on, heaven only knows. I was extremely shy of trying to speak, for I knew perfectly well that anything I had to say would be peppered with mistakes, and I am a lover of language. I love the process of choosing the precise word to bring out a subtle meaning, of turning a phrase in such a way as to shed a new light on a topic. And I knew that as far as the Welsh language was concerned, I could not say what I wanted to say but only what I was able to say. Luckily, a friend pushed me in the direction of a fortnight's crash course in Welsh at Aberystwyth, and it is perfectly true to say that I went in an English speaker and came out two weeks later speaking Welsh. Imperfect, halting and full of mistakes—but Welsh.

My husband came to pick me up at the end of the course, and on the way home in the car he said, 'Now you can make a real contribution to Wales. I hope before long you will be lecturing in Welsh and broadcasting in Welsh and adjudicating in Welsh!' I couldn't believe my ears. I only took the course so that I could hold a conversation with our friends, and here was this dreamer, fantasising about an impossible contribution in the Welsh language. And yet I, too, began to feel that perhaps I did have something to offer my adopted country.

In time everything he had hoped for came true. None of it was easy. By this time I was over 50 and learning took longer. So when I was asked to give a couple of radio broadcasts in Welsh about American folksongs, I spent hours not just preparing the material but saying the words over and over, so that my phrasing would sound natural and not stilted. Lecturing was even harder, for I have never liked to read my lectures but prefer, when possible, to talk naturally on the subject. After a period of doubt and trepidation I got the confidence to do that in Welsh. Most thrilling—and terrifying—of all was the invitation to adjudicate at the National Eisteddfod. With thousands listening in the pavilion, not to mention the thousands more who were tuned in on radio and television, the knowledge that all these people would be aware of an incorrect mutation or mangled word-order concentrated the mind wonderfully. But it was these very things that made me feel a part of the Welsh nation, instead of just a welcome guest.

I suppose if I say that the conscious decision to learn Welsh changed my life, some will snort in disbelief and turn to another page. But it is true. The Welsh language has given my life a focus it would not otherwise have had. When we lived in America during the 1950s I had an interesting and rewarding career in music, both teaching and performing. Our home was in a stimulating university town with a rich cultural life. But in a country of 250 million people, the kind of contribution I made could be made equally well by thousands of others. In Wales, with a long equally rich cultural tradition but only half-a-million Welsh speakers, any contribution is important. And so people are stimulated to use their gifts in every possible way. Consider the *llenorion* (a much more useful word than 'men of letters' and less pretentious than *litterateurs*). In England and America they tend to be compartmentalised into poets or essayists or novelists or biographers or scholars or political theorists or dramatists. But some of Wales' greatest literary figures are all of these things. Saunders Lewis is a case in point, and there are many, many others. The lively cultural activities in the Welsh language ensure the need for a wide variety of talents in as many different fields as possible.

I knew that any contribution I could make must be in the field of music and had I chosen to continue teaching and performing classical music, the Welsh language might well have been important to me merely as a means of conversation. But even before coming to Wales I had been aware of Welsh folksong. Until I began to learn Welsh, it was only the melodies that interested me; my knowledge of the words came through inexact translations that gave only the gist of the meaning. So the Welsh folksongs that caught my attention were the ones with attractive tunes, usually love songs. The result was that I passed over songs with a rather repetitive, chant-like melodic line made up of motifs, songs from a much older tradition. Some of these were connected with calendar customs such as the Mari Lwyd or Hela'r Dryw, both probably pre-Christian. Some were work songs such as the oxen-ploughing songs from

Glamorgan. Some were used for the competitive singing of *tribannau* at wedding celebrations. It wasn't until I had learned Welsh that I began to value these songs, not for their melodies, but for the combination of tune and words which opened a door on the Welsh past.

From an interest in the songs themselves came a wider interest in the people who collected them. Eighteenth-century antiquarian collectors like Iolo Morganwg and William Jones of Llangadfan jostle for attention with the generous Vicar of Ceri/Kerry, John Jenkins, who was almost contemporary with Beethoven, and whose splendid manuscript collection of Welsh folksongs now graces the National Library of Wales. Fifteen years after his death a gentlewoman, M. Jane Williams, from an old Welsh family renowned for its patronage of the Welsh bards, published a book of Welsh folksongs and dedicated it to Queen Victoria; a year later John Thomas (Ieuan Ddu), who supported the Chartists, also published a book of Welsh folksongs in order 'to make those same Airs a source of permanent delight to his countrymen'. In our century, Soley Thomas, a farmer, wandered the hills of north Cardiganshire collecting songs from roadside tramps or singers in taverns; and about the same time a schoolmaster, J. Ffos Davies, was calling at Dyffryn Aeron farms in south Cardiganshire, searching for songs. J. Lloyd Williams, Professor of Botany, applied his scientific training to the analysis of folksong and, as the first editor of the *Welsh Folksong Journal,* set the standard for all who followed in his footsteps. What all these individuals from differing backgrounds and eras had in common was their fierce love of Wales and pride in her culture.

These people have become as important to me as any of the figures from American history, as real as Daniel Boone or Patrick Henry. More real, in fact, because I have seen their manuscripts and letters which reveal something of their personalities. When I see the tunebook of one Anglesey fiddler, I note that he, like Shakespeare, couldn't make up his mind how to spell his name and so on the title page, which bears the date 1778, we find 'Maurice Edwards his Book' but a little further on, 'Morris Edwards his Hand'. Another eighteenth-century fiddler's tunebook, containing about 350 tunes to ballads, dances and songs for the *anterliwt* opens with a 16-page essay on fishing. I suspect he was a professional fiddler, who, when he wasn't playing minuets in the great houses or ballad tunes at the fairs, could be found down at the river indulging his passion for fishing.

Like all these, I too have a deep love of Wales and pride in her culture. In view of this, do I consider myself to be American or Welsh? Had you asked me this 15 years ago, my answer would have been unhesitating; I am an Amercian. Without qualification. Since I have learned Welsh, the answer isn't so easy. Yes, I am an American and will be all my life. But I am also a part of Wales now, not just a sojourner, and so there is a part of me that is inescapably Welsh. So much so that I think the next time we are in Powys I'll ask my husband to take me to see the grave of William Jones of Llangadfan.

COMING HOME
Sylvia Prys Jones

All my life I have been torn between the desire to belong and the desire to be different. It is these two conflicting traits of my personality, as much as any outward influences, which have been responsible for setting me upon my circuitous route to a discovery of Welshness.

I had always been aware of being Welsh. My father was born in Llanidloes, in mid-Wales: his father's family came from Goginan, near Aberystwyth and were Welsh-speaking. But his mother spoke little Welsh, and the family language was English. Llanidloes, even in the 1920s, was largely English-speaking, and my father's Sunday visits to China Street Welsh Baptist church did nothing to improve his Welsh, or nurture in him a fondness for nonconformist religion. But even as a a child he was aware of a sense of irritation that he, although Welsh, could not speak Welsh, and this never left him.

At the age of ten, he moved with his family to Hereford. My mother was Hereford born and bred (although of Welsh descent, like many Herefordians), and they met and married there at the end of the war. I was the youngest of their three children. But my father never forgot his Welsh origins, and never lost his desire to learn Welsh. His job took us to different parts of the country, and when I was seven we moved to Surrey.

I was a rather shy, solitary child, and I had found the move from the small primary school, which I had attended previously, to the rough and tumble of a large junior school to be quite traumatic. I was terrified of the noise of the playground and the boisterous older children. As it happened, the headmaster was from south Wales: I remember him singling me out for attention because I was Welsh. We even had the same surname: Morgan. The part-time teacher, Mrs. Thompson, was from the Rhondda. I adored her dark, graceful beauty, her soft, lilting, Valleys voice, and her quick smile (although all I can remember from her history lessons is the recipe for Baked Alaska!). One day, at lunch, I spilt my drink down my jumper. '*Mochyn!*' she laughed. Somehow or another I understood the word. It was probably the only Welsh word I knew. But the fact that she had spoken to me in Welsh gave me a warm, fellow feeling, as though we were sharing a secret.

Meanwhile my father, once a keen rugby player and now an enthusiastic spectator, had joined London Welsh Rugby Club. There, in the steamy, smoky atmosphere of the club room, full of beer fumes and *hiraeth*, he heard Welsh spoken around him for the first time in years. He had built a stereogram at home and found, by some freak of chance, that he could pick up Welsh-language radio programmes. His interest was rekindled and he made a start with learning Welsh, and also asked for a transfer to south Wales. I was ten when we moved to Cardiff.

Another school, another period of agonising shyness. This time the children mocked me for my posh English accent, and accused me of being a snob. It was not a happy time. But there I had my first Welsh lessons and discovered, for the first time, my natural aptitude for languages.

If I had been good at Chemistry, my life might have been different. But I was a linguist. At secondary school I studied Welsh, French, Latin and Greek, and found them all easy. Languages were my hobby, too. I studied Spanish in preparation for a continental holiday and, at the age of thirteen, managed to chat-up the waiters quite successfully. I had a bash at Esperanto, and a half-hearted attempt at Russian.

But it was Welsh which captured my interest, for it represented not just a language but an identity. I was a shy, diffident teenager: I had not coped easily with the frequent changes of school, and I found it hard when I was sent to boarding school at the age of eleven. My elder sister's education had been disrupted by our frequent moves, and my parents were determined that my brother and I should not suffer in the same way. But I found it a miserable, chafing existence, which only increased my sense of rootlessness and isolation. And yet I wanted to be different. The Welsh language gave me roots and a sense of direction, and also set me apart from the crowd.

I became a fervent Welsh nationalist. Two books which made a tremendous impression on me at that time were *The Welsh* by Wyn Griffiths, and *The Welsh Extremist* by Ned Thomas. In the newspapers, I followed the campaigns of the Welsh Language Society and the strange trial of the Free Wales Army. I became interested in Celtic countries generally and set about learning Breton, thus adding to my string of languages.

The strange aspect of this Welshness was that it was almost entirely an inward experience, a strange romantic notion in my imagination. It is hard for people today to realise how totally anglicised Cardiff was twenty years ago. There was only one Welsh primary school, no Welsh-medium secondary schools, no *Ysgolion Meithrin*, few Welsh-medium activities apart from those held by chapels, and little interest in learning Welsh. It is only during the last two decades that all these activities have blossomed like flowers in a desert. I knew hardly anyone who spoke Welsh, apart from my teacher and the little woman who used to come to wash supper dishes on a Sunday. Her name was Joan and she lived near Cardiff docks, and she and I would have long conversations in Welsh, to the intense irritation of the other girls.

My Welsh nationalism, too, had no political content. I had little grasp of political matters, and even less interest. To a young girl living in a select residential area of the city, and receiving her education in a rather posh boarding school, the whole flow of Welsh political history as a struggle against injustice, poverty and oppression, from the campaigns of Llywelyn, the last Prince of Wales, to the Rebecca riots, to the Treason of the Blue Books, made little sense to me.

Looking back at that period of fervent nationalism makes me blush, bearing, as it did, little relation to the Wales of reality. I knew little of the geography of Wales, its craggy, mist-wreathed peaks and lush, rolling valleys: I knew less of the people, of their struggle for survival and the preservation of their language. My Welshness was largely 'psychological': less of a response to the real, historical Wales than to a dim unperceived need within myself. It was, to a large extent, a foolish adolescent notion. Some of my contemporaries dreamt of pop stars, I dreamt of Wales. But even now, as I wince in memory, I wonder whether it was such a bad thing.

A few years ago the *Western Mail* ran an article about research which had been conducted at the University of Wales, Cardiff, into the reasons why adults learn Welsh. The researchers had, apparently, come to the conclusion that a large majority of the learners were people with certain weaknesses and hang-ups. Welsh was a crutch, it gave them the security of belonging. But is that such a tragedy? Is it a crime to want to belong, to be a part, to have roots? And if, in the process, we chance upon something of such immeasurable worth and beauty as the Welsh heritage, so much the better. And so I continued on my stumbling, bumbling road to a discovery of Welshness.

In one sense, I had arrived. Aberystwyth was, even then, famed as a Mecca for Welsh-speaking students. But it was a 'culture shock'. It was the first time that I had come into contact with Welsh-speaking Welsh people in any numbers, and I found it hard. My natural shyness was compounded by linguistic difficulties. My Welsh was correct but stilted, and I floundered in 'small talk'. I found it hard to understand some of the students, especially those from the north, with their guttural accents and unfamiliar dialect. Moreover, I found them distant and almost unfriendly: I wish now that I had understood more of the factors that had moulded their lives, the tiny close-knit communities, protective of their own kind and deeply suspicious of strangers. Accustomed to the easy politeness of urban life, I interpreted their reserve as unfriendliness, and was puzzled.

However, I settled down. My Welsh improved, and I held my own in a classful of native speakers. I was introduced to the glories of Welsh literature, the jewelled simplicity of Taliesin and Aneirin, Dafydd ap Gwilym's lyrical verses. I indulged my passion for languages by taking up Irish, but found it to be the only language which has totally defeated me. I specialised in philology and linguistics, and was enthralled by the unfolding history of the Welsh language, its versatility and vitality, from the earliest written records. More accustomed to the chaotic vagaries of English, I marvelled at the crystal clarity of Welsh, like a chiselled diamond. How could so many people treat it like a regional *patois*?

The social life of the Welsh students was a revelation. On the whole they were a wild lot. Many of them drank heavily, especially those from teetotal backgrounds. (I learnt to spot the ministers' sons lying comatose under the table.) But few of them dared tell their parents that they even darkened the door of a pub. It was my first introduction to that peculiarly Welsh brand of hypocrisy which stems from the worn trappings of a jaded nonconformism.

But when my fellow students weren't drinking, and sometimes when they were, they showed many talents. Many were excellent singers, others could play instruments, others could act. The Welsh hall of residence, Pantycelyn, had a fine choir which specialised in *cerdd dant,* the peculiarly Welsh art of singing poetry to a melody, while a contrasting melody is played on the harp. Brought up in the chapel and eisteddfod tradition, the students were natural performers and I remember many wonderful concerts, plays and folk evenings. I have never failed to be amazed at the ability of the Welsh in the performing arts, which tend to be the province of a favoured few in England.

Many students were poets and writers, too, and in the annual intercollegiate eisteddfod there were literary competitions as well as competitions for singing, recitation, instrumental performances and, of course, the chairing of the bard.

Aberystwyth brought other rich experiences. I made a fresh discovery of the Christian faith which had eluded me during the tedious cathedral services of my schooldays. This led me to read avidly about the Christian tradition of Wales, spanning the centuries from the early Celtic church through to Catholicism, to the Puritans and Nonconformists, and the revivals of the nineteenth and early twentieth centuries. This, coupled with the magnificent literary tradition which I had begun to discover, made me realise that Wales, although an insignificant little country, had a noble and mighty heritage. It was my responsibility, as a Welsh person and a Christian, to safeguard this heritage. I felt privileged, and inordinately proud.

While in Aberystwyth, I joined *Cymdeithas yr Iaith Gymraeg* (the Welsh Language Society) and attended rallies and protest marches. I learnt more of the geography of Wales, especially of the Cardiganshire area, with its gently undulating hills, its lush, fertile pastures and narrow leafy lanes. I have always considered it to be the most beautiful area of Wales, although perhaps the shimmering memories of college days have imbued it with a special beauty. Certainly the view of Aberystwyth as you come over the breast of Pen-glais hill on a fine summer's morning, the cluster of buildings softly blurred in the early mist and, behind them, Cardigan Bay sparkling in the sunlight, is one of the most magical in Wales.

In Aberystwyth, too, I discovered my own roots. Elderly relations, two brothers and a sister of my grandfather, live there. Their neat terrace house stood in one of the narrow, sloping streets near the station, full of genteel charm, with geraniums and bed-and-breakfast signs in the windows. I knew them vaguely and decided to visit them upon my arrival. They must have been rather surprised at their unexpected visitor, a skinny student in tight jeans, swathed in an Aberystwyth scarf, who spoke peculiar Welsh, but they greeted me with grave courtesy and ushered me into the dimly lit sitting-room. Thus began an unexpected friendship, which greatly enriched my Aberystwyth days. I would visit every fortnight or so, trying vainly to avoid mealtimes. But whatever time of day it was, the cloth would be spread and I would be regaled with strong tea, best boiled ham, bread and butter and home-made jam, and Aunty Maga's delicious cakes. The conversation would be about the family, local events and my college experiences, with Aunty Maga trying tentatively to fathom what I actually did there. Did I do much embroidery? She was a tiny woman, with quick movements, long jet-black hair coiled in a bun, and bright, grey-green eyes. She had kept house for her two batchelor brothers for many years and they lived together in tranquil harmony. I soon discovered that I was not their only visitor. They had always lived in the area and they had a wide circle of friends, who would call to pass the time of day and enjoy Maga's hospitality. Uncle Trevor, beside being the local postman, used to mend clocks and watches. He did it for love rather than for money, but he had many grateful customers. Some would consider that they lived a circumscribed life, but there was a richness and permanence about it that was like a balm to my spirit. They were never in a hurry, never too busy to talk, and they possessed a gentle, old-fashioned courtesy which I have since found is typical of so many Welsh people. I still call there now, although not so often. Only one brother remains, he is frailer, and Aunty Maga has a little white in her long black hair. But her eyes are as bright as ever, and her interest as keen. My debt to them is great. They have been, and still are, a link with my past.

I left Aberystwyth with my degree and for the next four years I led a nomadic life as a research student, going from Oxford to Brittany and back to Wales. It was a fascinating, often lonely time. It worried me that I was so happy in Oxford, speaking English and going punting on the Cherwell. After all, wasn't I the archetypal Welsh nationalist? I shared my worries with an Aberystwyth friend, and I have never forgotten his answer. 'Your reason for speaking Welsh,' he said, 'lies in Aberystwyth, not in Oxford.' It was like a neon light going on in my head. For the first time I made the connection. My Welshness wasn't simply an inward state. It was linked inextricably and inevitably with the land of Wales, its people, its language, its struggle for survival. From that moment on, my Welshness turned outwards.

In the fullness of time I returned to Aberystwyth, and thence, shortly, to north Wales, and married after a whirlwind romance. I suppose it was what I had always wanted, that tritest of trite desires, a husband and children, and a chance to put down roots. And so they came, the children—three boys, all named after family members—and the roots, in the little Welsh-speaking village of Waun-fawr, a long, untidy ribbon of a village perched on a shelf halfway down a mountain in Snowdonia. A grey, unprepossessing place perhaps, especially in winter when the rain beats incessantly on the grey-slate roof, and the air is dank and misty, with the clouds weighing low over the mountains. But on those rare, fine summer days, when the sky is a crystal blue and Moel Eilio and the Elephant Mountain shimmer indistinctly in the haze, there is no more beautiful place on earth. Snowdonia with its craggy, forbidding peaks and its glistening lakes, has a wild beauty all of its own: it is a wonderful place to live, to see the changing face of nature and the majestic presence of the mountains. But, for me, it has been of even greater significance. It has been the place where the bare bones of my Welshness have taken flesh, where my inward emotions have become wedded to the living, vital experience of life in a Welsh community. I have come to respect and love the local people: they can be prickly and suspicious of strangers, they lack smooth urban charm. But they are courteous and neighbourly, occasionally nosy, but always concerned and ready to help. I have been humbled, too, by the fact that the villagers, most of whom have never been near a university, can speak Welsh immeasurably better than I can, with a colour and fluency of idiom to which I can only aspire. Their cultural life is rich and varied, from the literary society to the poetry classes to the annual eisteddfod. They may watch 'Dallas', but they create their own culture in a way totally foreign to English people.

And so I have put down roots, and put a value on permanence. I look to the future, and to my children's future. I will never be one of the natives, but my sons are Waun-fawr boys. Children here are village property, known and loved by all. I see my sons growing up stable and confident, accepted for what they are by the close-knit village community. Moreover, I see them growing up as Welsh speakers. Some people are shocked that their English is so sketchy, and consider them deprived. But they are privileged. Their English will improve, but Welsh will be the language of their hearts, and they will have had a priceless gift, a bulwark against the flood of the monolithic, vapid Anglo-American culture which has swept through our country in recent decades. And finally, to the immigration: to the influx of English, attracted by the scenery, the outdoor life, the low house prices, and perhaps, deep down, by a sentiment as undefined and indefinable as that which first propelled me in the direction of Wales, the need to belong, and yet to be yourself. I cannot find it in my heart to think ill of them, and yet they are a real threat to the fragile fabric of life in the Welsh-speaking communities. My hope and prayer is that they will pause before they come, and consider whether they can, in any way, help these fragile communities, by learning their language, respecting their way of life, making their own unique contribution, and eventually, perhaps, discovering the precious heritage of Welshness for themselves.

'THE OUTER LOSS SHALL BE THE INNER GAIN'
A.M. Allchin

It must be almost thirty years since I first came to Wales. The astonishment of that first week of discovery is still with me. It was a case of love at first sight. It was a week of brilliant August weather in the early 1960s. My brother and I stayed almost by chance at Llanidloes (Lanidlowes, I called it then). We explored parts of mid-Wales and particularly the way over to Machynlleth.

It was a revelation of the beauty of the landscape, a vision of a world transfigured by light. At the time I knew nothing of the persistence of that vision of a transfigured world through the long centuries of Welsh poetry. For it was a revelation of the beauty of mid-Wales, it was also a revelation of the strangeness, the foreignness of the place. There was scarcely a name on a signpost which I could pronounce, let alone understand.

And behind my surprise and delight at all this, there was a question which kept coming back. How was it that I was so ignorant of this place? How could it be that I knew so little about it? After all I had had a good education; I was interested in the history of the island I live in. I knew something about England, and even a little about Scotland. But Wales—this was something new, something I had hever heard about. Here was a country with its own language, its own history, its own identity—and yet I knew nothing about it.

The discovery which began in that August week more than a quarter of a century ago has been going on ever since. It is a discovery which has involved a conversion on my part, a change of heart and mind, a change of perspective and understanding, which has opened my eyes to a great many things which I do not think I would otherwise have perceived. It has given me a new understanding of and a new love for my own country, England, and of the island in which we dwell, Great Britain, *Prydain Fawr*. Britain is a place which in those days I though of as more or less synonymous with England, but which I now know to be a larger, older, more complex phenomenon than that, an island which contains three nations not one, and the smallest of them has the longest and most continuous history of them all. For to recognise the separate existence of Wales and of the Welsh as a distinct people, with their own history and their own language, involves for an English person a distinct movement of conversion. For fifteen-hundred years we have been pretending that our Western neighbours are not there, or that if they are, they are beneath our contempt, not worth our attention.

The process of conversion is never altogether easy. At times it can be painful. It involves seeing things as they really are. In this case it involves, among other things, a new and more honest appraisal of the dark side of English history, of our capacity for destroying people and things almost without noticing that we are doing it, whether on the borders of Wales in the eighth and ninth centuries, or in the highlands of Scotland in the years after Culloden, or more recently in the middle of the nineteenth century in the famine years in Ireland. Imperial peoples carry with them heavy burdens, which grow all the heavier when they are not acknowledged. But the acknowledgement of guilt, particularly in a Christian context, brings with it liberation from guilt, and an immense sense of release and joy. It also brings a new capacity to see things and understand things. Repentance is not only or primarily about feelings, though feelings are involved in it. It is about a growth of consciousness, a new awareness of things as they really are, and that, again in a Christian context, means things in the God-given reality. For one whose faith centres on the cross, it is clear that even in the terrible things of life some hidden glory lies concealed. But that must not be said too easily. It is, I believe, the weight of deeply repressed and unacknowledged guilt which has made the English for so many centuries blind to what is actually there, for instance, in the splendours of Welsh poetry, or in the daily sensitivities of Welsh or Irish or Scottish people.

It will already be clear that for me the discovery of Wales and of Welshness has not been a kind of isolated hobby. I confess that at one moment, early on, I thought that that was what it would be; some people collect butterflies, I will take an interest in Wales. It is a journey of discovery which, for me, has been linked with two other journeys of the same kind, which have taken me into different parts of Europe, Scandinavia and the Balkans, and which have illuminated my discovery of Wales and been illuminated by it. I have no doubt that if I had journeyed more in the Third World, and had seen more of the end-results of colonisation, a similar process would have taken place there. But for me it has been Europe, and in particular the recognition that nations are not all of the same kind. There are different kinds of nations, nations whose existence and character is not necessarily and automatically to be measured by comparison with those of England.

The Scandinavian discovery is for me focused in Denmark, a country which I first visited as a schoolboy and which I have been visiting ever

13

Chapel Interior, Tythegston near Porth-cawl, by Suzanne Greenslade

since. Indeed, I first fell in love with Denmark when I was sixteen; I then fell in love with it again in my twenties, and recently, as my sixtieth birthday draws near, I discover that I have fallen in love with Denmark all over again; its people, its places, its language, its literature, its landscape and its seascape. I believe that every country is the most beautiful place in the world. Certainly one sees it so, when one falls in love, and if love is truth-telling as my faith tells me that it is, then I suppose it is part of the transcendent capacity of God that he can make a world in which every place and every person is unique, and uniquely lovely, a unique reflection of his infinite beauty and joy. The existence of a nation is something very special, something built up through the course of centuries. It results from a unique interpenetration through time which gives its particular character to each people in our world. As Solzhenitzyn remarks, 'Nations are the wealth of mankind, its generalised personalities; the least among them has its own unique colouration, harbours within itself a unique facet of God's design.'

In Denmark I learnt that a small nation is not the same as a large nation. There are advantages and disadvantages in both situations. In the twentieth century the devastating effects of the pretentions of large nations, particularly when they become imperial or totalitarian or both, have been so evident, that many people seem afraid to speak or think of nationality at all. But national identity will not go away, even though we pretend it is not there. Certainly the nationalism of large nations which define themselves mostly in terms of their economic and military power, their capacity to control and dominate other nations, is something which itself needs to be very strictly scrutinised and controlled. In the twentieth century it has had terrible effects on those who practise it— think only of Mussolini or Cecil Rhodes, not to speak of more serious and threatening figures—and on those who suffer it. But the situation of a small nation, whether of five million or two million or five-hundred thousand people is totally different. It cannot, even if it wants to, define itself in this way. Its economic power is very limited; its military power is negligible. It cannot dominate others; it has to learn to live in relationships of interdependence with them. Its definition and awareness of its national identity will necessarily be more internal than external, to do with shared memories and shared traditions, common experiences and common insights, usually conveyed and embodied in a shared language, whose very existence is often threatened in our age of mass-culture.

One of the advantages of a small nation is that it tends to maintain a greater sense of internal coherence and cohesion that a large one. It is less likely to break up into a series of distinct and mutually exclusive groups and classes. Even as a schoolboy I was aware in Denmark of being in a country where differences of social class were less divisive than they were and still are in England. Quite simply, where there are fewer people, people remain in closer contact with one another, the *people* remains a more easily experienced reality. Hence the impossibility of translating into English the Danish word *folkelig*. Of course it comes from *folk*; so it means popular. But it also means national; and then it can be used to mean popular in a positive sense which implies quality and character and excellence, as well as rootedness and earthiness and humour. It is a quality very familiar to anyone who gets inside Welsh-speaking Wales, notably evident, for instance, in the splendid mixture of people and events which goes to make up the National Eisteddfod. It speaks quite specifically of that interpenetration of people and place, which J. R. Jones saw as constitutive of a nation. It speaks of the way in which a particular people living in their own particular land have their own particular gift, a gift which is embodied in their whole history and experience as a people; something in which individuals share in a great multitude of ways.

In Christian terms this gift is seen as the gift and call of God, a gift which is to be shared with others, but not neglected or denied. Just as each person has his own gift, his own call, his own story, his own responsibility, his own insights, so it is with a whole people.

The fact that some nations are larger, richer, more successful and more powerful than others does not mean that they have a monopoly of those more inward gifts which go to sustain and build up national life; courage, wisdom, understanding, humour, resilience. Indeed, quite the reverse is the case, at least when the matter is seen in the perspective of the Gospels. Because small nations often experience oppression or defeat, they are likely to acquire gifts of insight and understanding which the powerful find it difficult to arrive at and which, from a Christian perspective, point towards the promises of the beatitudes, in which there is a blessing on those who mourn, those who are poor, who hunger and thirst after righteousness. The blessings of success and achievement are from this perspective always mixed blessings, often highly ambiguous. After Denmark's catastrophic defeat by Germany in 1864 and the loss of the southern provinces, the motto of the Danes, formulated by the agriculturalist Dalgas, became 'the outer loss shall be the inner gain'. We shall make up by the quality of our common life for the losses which we have sustained externally.

The life of a small nation, if it shuts itself in on itself, can become narrow and stifling. But this need not happen. Indeed, insofar as small nations are more likely than large nations to be aware of their need for relationship with others, it is not all that likely to happen. Certainly when the national identity is affirmed in a resolutely international way, as it was by Saunders Lewis in his pamphlet *Egwyddorion Cenedlaetholdeb*, 'Principles of Nationalism', at the foundation of Plaid Cymru, the danger of an inward-looking isolationism is greatly reduced. In the light of the development of organisations like the European Community it looks as though in many ways the smaller nations will be better equipped than the larger ones, which still hanker after total sovereignty, to flourish in the twenty-first century. What is made quite clear by the recent events in Eastern Europe, is that small nations have a remarkable resilience and staying power. We see this in countries like Lithuania, Latvia and Estonia. We see it in Georgia and Armenia. Human beings need to be able to locate themselves on the face of this planet, in terms of the history and experience of a particular people. To deny this is to stifle something vital for our human life.

If my discovery of Wales as a nation has been linked with my discovery of the nations of Scandinavia—and it is important to remember that that region contains peoples no more numerous than the Icelanders (250,000) or the Faeroese (55,000), Wales is really quite a large nation comparatively speaking—it has also been linked with my exploration of the Balkans and Eastern Europe, and particularly Romania. There I began to understand that there was not only a difference between large nations and small nations, but, to use the expression of an Irish bishop, between nations which have made history, and nations which have suffered history. There are countries who have usually been successful in war, and countries whose history is dominated by military disasters. One thinks of the centuries during which the people of Russia suffered under the Tartars, or of the period when Poland was divided and had apparently disappeared from the map of Europe. Such times impart a special quality to the awareness of national identity on the part of a whole people. When a country is without political independence, its people divided and dispersed, the maintenance of its national language becomes particularly important. The language holds the memory of the people, the memory holds their identity. So the Bishops of Poland could write in a Pastoral Letter of 1976, at a time when the present Pope was still Archbishop of Cracow,

> the cultivation of speech and language is the strongest spiritual bond which links each of us with the national community, with the community

of our native land. Those who are aware of the importance of this link, at home as well as in the emigration, have always taken to heart the need to defend the purity of the mother tongue and its zone of influence. This is verified by our experience as a nation in the time of slavery as well as in the time of dispersion and emigration.

They are words which, I suppose, would find an echo in the hearts of Welsh speakers as well as of those who speak minority languages throughout Europe.

But Romania is not only a country which has suffered periods of oppression and division. In the fifteen centuries between the fall of the Roman Empire and 1918 there was only one year, 1599-1600, when the three Romanian provinces were united and independent. For more than fourteen-hundred years, twice the time since the death of the last independent Prince of Wales, the Romanians maintained their sense of national identity without the help of any unified political structure. They are a people who have known constant invasion and political turmoil, constant oppression and exploitation. The tragic events of the days before Christmas 1989 were part of the texture of Romanian history. It was the language which mattered above all else in keeping alive amongst the people an awareness of *Romanitas* which has no parallel in Eastern Europe, and it survived for centuries by purely oral tradition. It was the language which conveyed a great wealth of *folkelig* culture, in the form of songs and stories, legends and proverbs, often growing up around the faith and piety of the Orthodox Church which was always identified with the life of the people. Here is a country held together by its mountains, a country in which popular faith, the national language and a constant resolution to snatch some inner victory out of external disaster, have conspired to sustain the identity of a people through centuries of oppression and defeat. It does not look like Wales, but its inner likeness made me at once feel at home.

I had the immense good fortune on my first visit to Romania to be able to see the country through the eyes of one of the finest theologians of our century, Fr Dumitru Staniloae, a man with a great love for his own country and for every country, a man in whom love and knowledge are combined in a way which is rarely seen in our broken world. From him I gained an understanding of the way in which the life and faith of the common people was at the heart of his own theological endeavour, a sense of the interpenetration between the piety of the monasteries, where he was always welcome, and the piety of the people of whom he was proud to be one, a sense of the marvellous interchange between earth and heaven, joy and tragedy, redemption and creation which marks the faith of the Romanian Church in a particular way. With him, I saw the meaning of the remark of another Orthodox priest, who said with great emphasis of the persecuted Christians in China, 'They will triumph through the power of the Crucified'. He spoke with the strength and conviction which comes from a people who have known centuries of oppression and persecution. If one wants to know how the miracle of Wales has come about, how the tradition has survived through the centuries against all odds, the experience of the peoples of Eastern Europe will help you to understand.

It may seem paradoxical that in an article in a book on 'Discovering Welshness', I have spoken so much about Denmark and Romania. But for the understanding of Wales, it is necessary to see that country in a European context, and to have standards of comparison other than those of England. Seen in the kind of context which I have sketched here, things look very different. The *folkelig* culture of Wales, as expressed for instance in its hymns, no longer looks so strange as it does from a purely English viewpoint. The Danes are as surprised as the Welsh by the general English failure to take hymns seriously as a part of the literary and religious heritage of their nation. Seen against the number of speakers of Icelandic or Faeroese, the number of speakers of Welsh no longer seems so unimpressive. Perhaps, too, we learn from such figures to escape from the tyranny of numbers, which have very little to say about the quality which can inform a minority culture. Seen in the context of the peoples of Eastern Europe, the histories of the Celtic peoples no longer look so lonely or so isolated. People who have suffered history feel the presence of the past for good and ill, more acutely than peoples who have made history. Hence historical events, which to the English seem remote, are not remote to the people of Wales, or Greece or Serbia. The presence of the saints is all around us. We see at the two extremities of Europe, to the east and to the west, to what a degree the message of the resurrection, the triumph over death through death, can penetrate into the history and experience of whole peoples.

In some ways I should have liked in these pages to have expatiated on some of the many places and people whom I have discovered in the course of my discovery of Wales. There are the figures from the past who have particularly captured my attention, St Melangell and St Dwynwen from the Celtic ages, Dafydd Nanmor from the golden century, Edmwnd Prys and John Davies of Mallwyd from the period of the renaissance and the reformation, Ann Griffiths and her mentor Thomas Jones of Denbigh from the second generation of the Methodist revival. There are figures from the present whom I have had the privilege and joy of coming to know, most of them still alive, but some no longer present in this world, notable among them, Euros Bowen, priest, poet and scholar; David Jones, that wonderful interpreter of the primary place of Wales within the island of Britain; and above all, John Saunders Lewis, a man of true magnanimity, great in heart, in mind, and in spirit. I should have liked to have written about some of the other writers of the middle of this century, and in particular two of them, whom I feel I have come to know through knowing those who were their friends, Gwenallt and Waldo Williams. Such men have been the glory of our island in the last generation, men who have refashioned a vision of their nation, and sung the praise of God in face of all the darkness and despair of our times. If I began to speak of the places I have discovered in Wales, the little hidden churches, the islands and the valleys, the mountains and the Hills, how could I ever stop? Let two places stand for all, the Church of St Brynach at Nanhyfer (Nevern) in the south, and Ynys Enlli, Bardsey Island, the island of the saints in the north. For it is by the prayers of the saints that a people is, in the end, preserved from the disasters which follow on success, no less than from the more obvious disasters incumbent on defeat. And it is the saints, or in Gwenallt's poem, St David himself, who speak to us 'of the person, the family, the nation and the society of nations, and the cross which prevents us making any of them into a God'. For the richness of the vision which the saints of Wales convey from the beginning till today, how can I fail to be unendingly grateful?

THE MAN WHO WAS FRISKED OF HIS CHINA RUGBY BALL
Jon Dressell

When I first came to Wales, more than quarter of a century ago, I brought with me, unavoidably, certain preconceptions. As a person with a strong familial connection with Wales I was hardly your average American visitor, but, in a sense, my preconceptions were those he might have had.

The average American is of course a creature of myth and statistics, but insofar as he might be said to have a sense of Wales at all, he has acquired it by watching returns of the 1939 film of 'How Green Was My Valley' on late-night television. He thus believes that all the Welsh live in terraced houses on hillsides, and that all Welsh men wear woollen caps and mufflers and like to sing on their way to and from the coal mines. He believes that the Welsh bear up nobly under conditions which are often harsh, that the men enjoy their pint and like to smoke their pipes, and that they are looked after tolerantly and lovingly by formidable women. He believes that the skies of Wales are sombre, and that the dominant colour of the landscape is grey. After all, Hollywood blew its technicolour budget for 1939 on 'Gone With the Wind'.

There had been little in my boyhood in the steel-milling town of Granite City, Illinois, to disabuse me of this kind of romanticized Valley-centric view of Wales. Although my Welsh grandfather was a steelworker and not a coal miner, he loved to sing, and indeed was a leader of church and masonic choirs and an organizer of eisteddfodau. He liked his pint, and always took beer with him in his lunch pail to the mill. His working life was hard, shot full of strikes as American labour struggled to organize itself in the early part of this century. He was a union man to the end, and led a successful campaign to prevent the Carnegie Foundation from endowing the Granite City Public Library with what he called 'blood money'.

And he was indeed married to a formidable woman, whom he had met years before in a mill at Llanelli, where she had carried lunches to the men. When he was out on a year-long strike in Indiana, which ultimately cost him his job and forced him to move westward to Illinois, my grandmother not only kept the household together but managed the family's meagre finances so resourcefully that my grandfather was able to attend a music course at a college in Michigan. She baked bread and made welshcakes every day of her life, brewed a little dandelion wine on occasion, and loved her children, and grandchildren, in a smotheringly, over-protective way. I was known to her as 'Sioni Bach', and was in the fourth grade of primary school before I went a full week without being kept home a day because of a suspicious sneeze.

Granite City was not the Rhondda of course, but still, had I had novelistic inclinations, I might have attempted an epic with a title such as 'How Green Was My Prairie', for certainly the industrial landscape which surrounded me as a boy could have come straight from south Wales, and the gritty, grey and grimy town stood in sharp contrast to the green farmland all around it. At any rate, I was quite prepared to see and experience a certain kind of Wales when I emerged for the first time from the Severn tunnel on a grey November day in 1961. My wife and

I, married just two years, had gone into hock in order to take a fling at Europe before having our first child. We had visited seven great cities—Madrid, Rome, Florence, Venice, Vienna, Berlin and Paris—in nineteen days, and had wound up in London, where we decided to make a one-day excursion to Wales. It may have been a kind of guilt, penitential impulse after our hedonistic enjoyment of high civilisation on the Continent. That, or something else. Whatever it was, we were off to Paddington in the morning.

It was raining as we pressed our noses against the window of our pre-Intercity compartment and looked out at Wales through a swirling Celtic mist, which was enhanced by the effusions of our steam locomotive. Sure enough, there *were* terraced houses on the hillsides in the distance. And as we rolled slowly into Newport, I got a close-up view of my first Welshman on home soil. He was craggy of countenance, and looked for all the world like Donald Crisp. He was wearing a woollen cap and muffler, had just emerged from a pub, and was engaged in trying to relight his pipe.

As the train clattered on, we viewed the sooty backsides of what we presumed to be the houses of singing workers, brightened here and there by gardens in which late flowers bloomed. Defiant Welsh washing flapped lyrically in the rain. Now and then a formidable woman materialized in a window. At Port Talbot I experienced a near-religious sense of awe, for there, set down by the sea, was The Granite City Steel Company, only it was called The Steel Company of Wales. 'Benjamin Jones, we are here,' I whispered, as if to my grandfather's hovering ghost.

At Llanelli we were met by half a dozen cousins, who had never seen anyone from the American branch of the family, but who knew all about us from correspondence which my grandmother, and later my mother, had maintained over the years. The last visit by anyone from America had in fact been sixty year before, in 1901, when my grandmother had come back for six months with two of her small children. The cousins excitedly informed us that the night before my grandmother had left to return to the United States in 1901, a certain lumberyard in Llanelli had burned, and that the night before our arrival it had, portentuously, burned again. We repaired to a family house on Copperworks Road near the station, to discuss this omen and whether we owed the lumberyard proprietors an apology.

We spent the afternoon trading family history, drinking tea, eating welshcakes, and taking a short walking tour of Llanelli. It was brought home to me, sitting in that modest parlour in Copperworks Road, a coal fire in the grate, the life of the street bustling by outside, just how Welsh my early family life in America had been. These people looked, talked, gestured, expressed, exclaimed, just like my grandmother and her Welsh cronies had. Their capacity for self-ironic humour, their sense of the ridiculous, was as I remembered hers, and as I felt it has been, at least partially, inculcated in me.

When we left that evening to return to London, and thence to America on the following day, I felt that some profound reconnection had been made. And in my raincoat pocket, bulging significantly, was its symbolic manifestation: a china rugby ball, a bank for coins, emblazoned with the logo, 'Llanelli R.F.C.'. I had admired it on the parlour mantel, and of course a cousin had immediately declared it mine. At customs in New York I was unceremoniously yanked (no pun intended) from line by a couple of steely-eyed federal agents and taken to an interrogation room, leaving my twenty-one year old bride behind me in a state of near-hysteria. The humourless G-men were polite, but firm. I had an ominous bulge in my raincoat pocket. I might be smuggling drugs.

When I produced the china rugby ball they exchanged knowing glances, and betrayed just the slightest hint of disappointment when removal of the rubber stopper at its bottom produced no flow of marijuana or cocaine. I was returned to my wife with perfunctory apologies. There had been something potent in that silly ball, though, and they had been right, as agents of Yankee authority, to be suspicious of me, for I have been a different kind of American since.

After that whirlwind one-day visit in 1961 I decided to come back to Wales for a summer holiday just as soon as we could afford it. It took three years to save the money, and in 1964 we came for three weeks. After a reunion with the cousins in Llanelli, we took in the National Eisteddfod at Swansea, and then, like all good Americans with an interest in literature, made a pilgrimage to Laugharne. There we stumbled upon a week-long festival involving nightly productions of *Under Milk Wood* which, in the 1960s and early 1970s, was a triennial event.

We went to the play several nights running, got to know members of the cast and crew, and drank with them after the performances at parties that lasted nearly till dawn. Afterwards, full of beer and *hwyl*, we would make our way slowly along the cliff walk from the Glan-y-Môr Club, past Dylan's little blue shed, and down his 'starless and bible-black' lanes to the town's main street below. I felt at those times that in some magical and romantic way the tentative reconnection I had made on the

November day three years before had been profoundly solidified and extended.

Beer and *hwyl* can work temporary wonders, of course, but something real and deep tugged at me nonetheless. We came again in 1967, this time with our two small children in tow, and spent the entire month of August in Laugharne. We found that *Under Milk Wood* was being done both in English and, as *Dan y Wenallt,* in Welsh adaptation. I don't know how Dylan would have felt about it, but both the performances and the social activities which surrounded them seemed to me to take on an added significance, and intensity, because of that.

Laugharne is an extremely interesting place, but it has never been known for being a stronghold of the Welsh language. I am probably one of the few people alive whose desire to learn the language was given a quantum boost by spending a week there. That is what happened, though, thanks to our Milk Wood/Wenallt friends. During our visit three years earlier I had come to realize that the Welsh language was still a living force and had not, as I think I had subconsciously assumed, died with my grandmother in 1950. I had found words and phrases from my childhood coming back to me then, and had taken back with me from the eisteddfod field several children's books and a *Geiriadur Bach.* Learning Welsh in Saint Louis is a solitary enterprise indeed, but I had made some progress. Enough, evidently, that some of our friends felt I would benefit from an experience of more total immersion. After the Laugharne productions had ended, we were urged to come along for a couple of days to the Bala National Eisteddfod.

There were no rooms to be had in Bala, so we stayed in Dolgellau and drove back and forth. We were, like any reasonably sensitive visitors, impressed by the aesthetic grandeur of the north. It reminded me of parts of Colorado, made more beautiful, if anything, by a sense of greater long-term human involvement. More than this, however, I was impressed by a sense of being in the Welsh-speaking heartland, with all that that implied in terms of a bimillenial accretion of history, legend and custom, and continuity of linguistic and cultural identity. Here was a Wales beyond anything hinted at in my boyhood experience, and which my prior experiences in the south had only just begun to prepare me to confront: a Wales that lived and spoke its own language, a Wales, or so it seemed to me at the time, that still possessed a deep, and unfractured, integrity.

This was a naïve reaction, and I came to realize that in time. I came to realize that those forces—social, linguistic, economic, psychological— which so threaten the Welsh identity are pervasive, and respect, ultimately, no territorial sanctuaries. It was not a realization easily gained. To come to this kind of understanding of Wales requires, it seems to me, a considerable investment of time and sensibility on the part of an outsider, even an outsider of more than casual Welsh connection. In my case it has involved not only spending considerable time in the Welsh-speaking heartland on subsequent visits, but finally committing myself, personally and professionally, to residence in it for much of each year.

That part of the heartland (hinterland, some would say, which seems to me a central question in terms of Welsh identity) to which I have committed myself for the better part of two decades now has turned out to be in Dyfed rather than Gwynedd. In 1973 I was able to come to Trinity College, Carmarthen, on an academic sabbatical, and lecture on American literature for a term. Out of that grew the programme for American students at Trinity, which I have directed since 1976. Had things happened differently, I can conceive of having done something similar in north Wales, but as it is, working in Carmarthen and living in Llansteffan has been, for me, a kind of fortuitous compromise. I have been able to live in close proximity to that part of industrial south Wales out of which my immediate Welsh ancestors came, and yet be part of a community which remains, however tenuously, in *Y Fro Gymraeg*.

I do not see it as a matter of having your cake and eating it. For me it is a matter of seeing, and feeling, Wales as a whole. For if my experience in the Welsh heartland has taught me that it is the whole of Wales that is under cultural assault, it has also taught me that any 'whole of Wales' that is worth defending has got the heartland at its core. I think that those who emphasize south Wales sometimes overlook this. Much would prefer that Cardiff and the Valleys had never happened, but the reverse of this kind of cultural myopia also exists, and seems to me a more potentially fatal affliction than its opposite.

Even discounting the 'How Green Was My Valley' factor, coming back to industrial south Wales had about it for me a quality of *deja vu*. I was, after all, coming to 'American Wales' from 'Welsh America', from one coalfield-steelworks community to another. If I were to recite to you the history of Granite City, Illinois, you could almost close your eyes and think I was telling you the story of industrial south Wales. It is all there, the establishment of basic industry in an area which had been agrarian, the influx of labour from surrounding rural areas, and from further, and further, away; the boiling of the melting pot, the struggle of labour for decent wages and conditions, and for education; the strikes, the periods of prosperity, the depressions, the long decline, the lay-offs and plant closures, even the advent of the Japanese.

In saying this, I in no way intend to demean the experience of industrial south Wales. It has been the experience of my family, on both sides of the Atlantic Ocean, which is to say that it has been an essential experience of humankind in Western industrial society in our time. But it has not been the only experience, let alone the whole.

That seems an obvious thing to say, but I think that those of us whose background is urban and industrial sometimes need to be reminded that life in the agrarian world is with us still, and possesses a dignity and validity of its own. Further, we need to acknowledge that a sense of the wholeness of Wales, or the wholeness of America, must involve an understanding of the relation of the urban and rural worlds to each other, both in terms of their contemporary interaction and in terms of the ways in which the older agrarian world has shaped certain attitudes and values, without which life in the urban situation might be humanly intolerable.

I am speaking of those attitudes and values which derive from seeing life primarily in terms of smaller social units. The importance of this seems to me increasingly apparent as we move from the industrializing experience into the post-industrial era. I would suggest, in fact, that the degree to which any group of people has survived the distintegrating pressures of the industrial experience is related to the degree to which they have held to the smaller view of life, which is essentially a legacy from the agrarian world.

My attraction to life in *Y Fro Gymraeg* has caused me to think about things such as this but I recognise, of course, that there is nothing unique to Wales in it. Writers as diverse as William Faulkner and Saul Bellow have brooded about it in their novels, from the perspective of rural Mississippi on the one hand, and the Jewish ghettoes of Chicago and New York on the other.

Yet Welshness does involve for me this sense of community which derives from what I have called the smaller view of life. And Wales seems to me fortunate in that, like a few other nations, it is small enough in terms of both territory and population to function as a genuine national community, though the extent to which it will do so remains to be seen. Beyond this, however, are matters of time and place which, to me, give the Welsh experience its truly special quality.

Wales saturates the consciousness with a sense of time. The Welsh, and their predecessors, have continuously occupied this piece of peninsular earth in the far west of Britain for so terribly long. The physical reminders of this are everywhere—the megalithic burial chambers, the standing stones in fields, the earthen ramparts of hill forts, the medieval ruins. More important still, the Welsh language survives, not as a relic but as a link with the past in much of its immensity. To live always with such a sense of an extended past around and behind one is to live in a world which, the dissent of Caradoc Evans noted, ultimately insists on humility, on a deeply sympathetic human perspective; a world which will not long support temporal, or metropolitan, arrogance.

Bound up with this is the nature of the place. We live, out here, not just in a place which is incredibly ancient in terms of human involvement with it, but which has about it physically an ultimacy and inescapability. In the age of the jet plane and satellite television this may seem a naïve thing to say, but only if one never thinks in metaphoric terms. Rimmed by the sea, hemmed in by its hills and mountains, Wales constantly reminds me, in a metaphoric way, of the spiritual truth that we must take a stand, finally, and face the limitations of the human condition, must live with other mortals in a world that has an end. The world is round, and Wales is not its literal end; beyond the western sea are Ireland and the Americas, and to the east and south are England and Europe, where other human beings must do the same thing. Yet I have been to no other place where the land lies in metaphoric relation to the human condition as resonantly as in Wales. Other such places there no doubt are, but Wales, for me, will have to do, and does.

'SAESON YW EI RIENI, 'CHI'N GWELD ...'
'His parents are English, you see ...'
John Geraint

I felt as uneasy and as angry when I first heard my background misrepresented in this way as a I was when I was first invited to contribute to a book about 'discovering Welshness'. True, Mam and Dad don't speak the Welsh language, but they would be annoyed in the extreme if you tried to tell them they were English, and puzzled by the suggestion that they needed to 'discover Welshness'.

Porth Town Centre, Rhondda, by David Bailey

There *was* a certain amount of Welsh spoken around the house. My grandfather was reasonably fluent, and sometimes, when his elder brother visited us from Tonyrefail, I'd hear a sentence or two exchanged before they turned, quite naturally, back to English. When I went out to play, of course, that was all English . . .

'Brynli saw a bwgibo up the gwli last night.'
'Don't talk twp, myn, he was up there with Delun.'
'Hey! Gis an ansh of your apple . . .'

Well, we *might* have said things like that. More likely, we'd have said 'stupid', and more likely it was Paul who was up to no good with Charmaine in the back lane. But we weren't so stupid that we didn't know what *'twp'* meant, and those Welsh names weren't foreign to us either. After all, we played in Hendre-cafn and Penmaes-glas, on Craig-yr-eos and Carncelyn. So it always strikes me as odd when I think about those childhood friends in Pen-y-graig—Dilwyn Jenkins and Sidney Reynolds, Gareth Richards and Paul Dodd—and realise that they're baldly counted now among the *non*-Welsh speakers in every census, as though they had as little contact with the language as the latest-coming factory-manager or retiree to move in from across the border. And it drives me to distraction when I read yet *another* letter in the *Western Mail* saying they can't be Welsh unless they speak Welsh, as though their accents, their background, their culture, their history simply didn't exist.

To be fair, you get a lot less of that nowadays. The zealots are still around, but mainstream nationalism has become much more liberal and talks about building bridges, and what we've got in common. Some time ago I heard some of the leaders of our national party declaring on television, 'The problems of Welsh-speaking youth and the problems of English-speaking youth are the same!' And only the other day I caught a key figure in the language movement using that very same phrase. Someone really ought to tell them that yuppie money buying up the local housing stock is not a problem that greatly afflicts the unemployed school-leavers of Treherbert or Penrhiwceiber.

I know, I know; up to a point they do have a decent argument—that the economic dominance of the south-east of England and the lack of social investment in 'peripheral' regions can debilitate and destabilize communities right across Wales. But the differences of communal needs, and the varieties of Welsh experience, demand an understanding much more profound and an analysis far more rigorous and honest before they can all be subsumed into nationalist rhetoric. Nationalist politicians looking for a nation to represent, might recognise that Dilwyn and Sidney, Gareth and Paul have a right to expect true solidarity, not sloganising. And perhaps the language activists would do well to remember that linguistic communication is about comprehension as well as expression, about listening as well as talking.

As for me, an educational system devised by the English (and embraced enthusiastically by the Welsh) gradually began to take me away from many of those boyhood friends. At grammar school, encouraged by some brilliant and deeply-committed teachers, you might say that I started to discover *their* sort of Welshness. I kissed my first girl on the back seat of the bus home from a weekend in the *Urdd* centre in Llangrannog; I camped out for the first time on the eisteddfod field at Rhuthun. The language became important for me as a kind of *re*-discovery. Fragments of hymns, remembered from my grandfather's singing, became comprehensible for the first time. Everyday phrases, misty yet familiar, came into sharper focus. And, eventually, my bookish, schoolboy-Welsh was transformed into a living language for me by a month spent working on a farm in west Wales. But, paradoxically, in what some might see as the culminating moment of my discovery of my own national heritage, that false, revealing phrase was used as an explanation to a neighbouring farmer of my not-quite-native command of the language:

'*Saeson yw ei rieni, 'chi'n gweld . . .*'

For me, fluency in Welsh has been enriching and enabling, a wonderful gift which others worked hard — personally and politically —to give me, and for which I hope I shall always be grateful. Certainly, I hope and expect to pass the gift on to my children. But I cannot say that in gaining the language I have discovered Welshness, or that Dilwyn Jenkins, Sidney Reynolds, Gareth Richards, Paul Dodd—who were never given the educational advantages that I was—have yet to discover it. I suppose I might say that I began by being Welsh and discovered the world. I suppose I might find it useful to talk of 'Welshnesses', as one nationalist politician has done, and say that I was born into one sort, and discovered another. But I've just finished Primo Levi's sober and chilling account of his time in the fascist death-camps of Auschwitz. I think I'll leave national characteristics alone for a while. I prefer to talk about people. I've an inkling that Dilwyn and Sidney, Gareth and Paul do, too.

A LANGUAGE TO LIVE BY
John Gillibrand

I, like so many other Welsh learners, come from a totally English background, being born in Eccles, Manchester, and spending all my early years there, until leaving in 1979 to study History at university. At an early age I joined the choir at the local parish church, and very soon afterwards the idea came to me that I wanted to be a priest in the Church of England. From time to time I thought of doing other things, but this vocation to the ministry stayed with me from a very young age. It never occurred to me that if I became a priest I would find myself exercising my ministry outside an English context. However, in the late 1970s, roughly coinciding with my departure for college, my parents began to develop business interests in the area of Port Dinorwic (Y Felinheli), and from that time onwards I found myself spending much of the college vacations in Wales. The Welsh language was, at this point, a totally new discovery: I remember as a teenager examining the bilingual signs in Caernarfon, completely unaware that Welsh was a living language. I came to the conclusion that they must have been set up by the local authority to interest and amuse the tourists who visit the castle in such numbers.

After leaving college, I trained to be a teacher. The Anglican Church in England and Wales tends to urge young people who are seeking ordination to broaden their experience of the world before they embark upon a career in the full-time ministry. It is difficult to think of someone preaching about God's love for the world, if they do not know very much about the world in the first place! In the year after college my experience was broadened immeasurably by a teaching practice in a London comprehensive school. It is of some significance that Welsh uses the same word for teaching and learning, *dysgu*. I was supposed to be teaching the boys in that school, but I am sure that I learnt far more from them than they ever did from me. After finishing my teaching practice I began to look for a teaching post, with no particularly strong feelings about where I wanted to live. I applied for posts as far apart as Edinburgh, Manchester, Liverpool and the Home Counties. Yet the school which offered me a job was, by chance, in Wales: Hawarden High School in Clwyd. Hawarden is hardly in the depths of the countryside, yet this was to be my first small taste of rural life. The classroom in which Religious Studies were taught overlooked some fields at the back of the school. I taught a class in that room shortly after my arrival and, that evening,

31

rang a friend in London to say that the new school was so far out in the country that we could see sheep from the classroom windows!

Hawarden is a heavily anglicised village, on the border with England. Yet it was at this school that, for the first time, I came into contact with people for whom the Welsh language was significant. To members of the Welsh department the teaching of Welsh was more than simply a job. It was also a personal commitment. It is necessary for any teacher to be committed to his or her subject: what it was necessary for me to work out was why the Welsh language attracted such a commitment, especially in such an anglicised area.

Such questions had to wait for an answer until a few years later. In the mid-1980s my father retired and purchased a retirement home in Tregarth, near Bangor. Shortly after this an interview was arranged for me with the Bishop of Bangor, the Right Reverend Cledan Mears, so that we could discuss the possibility of my entering the ministry or, rather, of embarking upon the selection process. This was necessarily a searching interview, and it included a question which is asked—in keeping with the Bishop's policy—of all those who seek Holy Orders in the Church in Wales who are not Welsh speakers: 'Are you willing to learn Welsh?' I was in no doubt as to how to answer this question, 'yes'. Yet, at the beginning, I regarded learning Welsh as more or less a practical matter. I was, by now, aware of the high proportion of the population of Gwynedd who are Welsh speakers, so it would clearly make my ministry in such an area easier if I had some command of the language.

Having passed through the different stages of the selection process I embarked on the three-year training course. Ironically, I was sent to follow a course in England, at Saint Stephen's House in Oxford. The then principal of the college, David Thomas, was the son of a former Bishop of Swansea and Brecon. The first two years at the college were academically highly pressurised, but at the end of the second year the bishop enabled me to go on a two-week residential Welsh course in the Extra-Mural Department of Bangor University. I had been learning a few Welsh words over the previous two years, but this course gave me the grammatical knowledge and, above all, the confidence to put some of these words together in sentences, and thus to begin to make simple conversation. Perhaps the biggest step for any learner is to begin a conversation with a tentative '*Sut 'dach chi?*', and then to continue the conversation—in some form—from this starting point. I found that by moving quite rapidly from Welsh to English and back again, it soon became easier and easier to talk about simple things.

It could be said that it was not I who made the effort to learn Welsh, but the people of Dolgellau who made the effort to teach Welsh to me. I have reason to be grateful to them, for the learning of Welsh has opened up whole new fields of experience and activity. I also started, for two hours on a Monday night, to teach Welsh to a group of about fifteen to twenty other learners, most of them English people who, like myself, had just come to the area and who were willing—more than willing, eager—to learn Welsh. A number of chapels in the area were also kind enough to extend to me the invitation to preach, and to lead their services.

The whole experience of 'discovering Welshness' raises questions concerning cultural identity of the most profound kind. Some learners, especially those who attain a certain degree of fluency, adopt the strategy of identifying themselves whole-heartedly with the Welsh-speaking community. The fluent Welsh learner, of whatever background, is taken to be a Welshman or Welshwoman. The question has, on occasions, been asked of me: 'You were an Englishman, weren't you?' My own non-Welsh-speaking twin-brother describes me in all seriousness to his friends as a Welshman. There is more than an element of truth in all this. Anyone who, as a result of learning Welsh, can sometimes more quickly recall the Welsh word than the English word for an object, has to regard him- or herself in a very real sense as Welsh. By coming to Wales I have discovered a national identity. Yet, it would be truer to say that in coming to Wales I have discovered in myself not one national identity but two. While living in England I was aware of that age-old phenomenon of nationalism, but regarded it as a bad thing, representing the feelings of superiority which one nation feels in relation to other nations. Only on arrival in Wales did I come into contact with people who regarded their own land, their own nation and their own people with pride, but not necessarily in relation to other nations. Rather, their own nation and culture had an absolute value and did not need to be compared to others. Thus the Welsh people taught me how to value my own culture for its own sake. This is why I speak of the discovery of two national identities: fundamentally the discovery of a Welsh identity went hand in hand with the rediscovery of an English identity.

In my upbringing in England, a sense of English identity remained deeply submerged for a variety of reasons. Firstly, on account of the American popular culture which has so heavily overlaid any sense of 'Englishness' in England. Secondly, there was no other culture or nation against which I could measure my Englishness. A national culture consists of a whole complex of ways of thought and ways of doing things which are taken for granted. They remain as unconscious assumptions of a way of life, unconscious, that is, until they are brought into direct contact with another culture. My increasing awareness of Welsh culture thus heightened my sense of English culture. The whole process poses a problem. Is it in the nature of a culture, be it English, Welsh or some other national culture, to be all-consuming? Culture, by its very definition, is a specific way of life. There is no aspect of life which any one culture leaves untouched. Therefore, to hold two cultures within one personal life is bound to generate tension. This is a problem which all Welsh learners face. It is a problem faced by all those whose life story leads them into the transitional area between one culture and another: how to live on the boundary between two cultures, and to participate fully in both, while allowing this to be a creative rather than a destructive experience?

Non-Christian readers will have to forgive me for turning to theology to explain why the experience has not been a destructive one. Christianity manifests itself in various cultural forms, tied to specific societies: the Catholicism of, say, Spain or Ireland, the Lutheranism of parts of Germany, the Anglicanism of England, the Nonconformity of Wales. Christianity in these forms represents the assumptions of a more or less dominant sector within these societies. Yet, essentially, the message of Christianity is a trans-cultural one. It has shown itself repeatedly throughout history to be portable from one society to another. Thus, if I am asked, as a Christian priest, how I unify the two cultural identities which I have discovered, the answer would be that whether I preach in Welsh or in English, to a Welsh- or English-speaking community, the message is the same.

THE IMPORTANCE OF IDENTITY
Patricia Elton Mayo

As long ago as the winter after the war my husband and I were lent a house in what was very much Welsh Wales: Llyndy, a house by a lake near Aberglaslyn. We had always been moved, when on holiday thereabouts, by such amazing physical beauty, but it was in that winter we understood Wales was much more than a place on a map. I was often alone. My husband was working in London and came down when he could. There was no electric light; there were lamps, candles and wood fires. As dusk fell, sheep would pass the windows on their way down from the hills for the night, and in the early morning would file back to their daytime pastures. I had never known such beauty and such peace, and perhaps in this silence my heart opened to the real Wales.

I made friends with the local farmers, Welsh-speaking all, and soon became conscious of a great divide between their basic outlook and the anglicised assumptions of the local gentry, however long they had lived in Wales. The girl who worked in the house had a wonderful voice. Making beds she would stop and dash to the kitchen, new words for a song to be written down before they were forgotten. I do not know whether watching television has been a discouragement, but in those days there were wonderful local concerts: local voices, local talent, love of making and listening to music written locally, an atmosphere of gaiety and happiness that could last until two in the morning. The gardener had worked in the quarries at Blaenau Ffestiniog where life was very hard. They were 'allowed' home at weekends. These people were gentle and fatalist, and totally lacking in consciousness of class. They were very un-English!

I now live in the border country which is not very Welsh. I wish it were more so because I miss the friendliness and the intellectual curiosity of the Welsh people. When we first came to this part of the Marches twenty-five years ago, there was a certain shame attached to admitting to being Welsh. Everyone was really very English, which was patently incorrect. There was a strong substratum which was not. A Welsh name 'ap Ynner' had become the anglicized 'Bunner'. Our local farmer would not admit that his family had spoken Welsh, although he came from a very Welsh-speaking village. Now things have changed. It is rather fashionable to talk or to learn the language.

There is sometimes a residual irritation on the part of the incomer to Welsh Wales, as opposed to the Border, as to why people should still wish to speak Welsh. Yet Freud believed the loss of cultural roots to be equivalent to loss of memory. It is obvious that Welsh is unlikely to be the vehicle for international commerce, but to speak English is no reason why Welsh cannot also be spoken. To lose a parent language is to lose a part of cultural and historic identity.

Both the English and the French have, in the past, been intolerant of their minority languages. Richelieu invented the word 'patois', implying a dialect spoken in 'patelins'—small local areas. Some of these 'patois', like Occitan, were older literary languages than French. The English and the French used to punish children overheard speaking

Welsh or Breton, respectively, at school. Happily this is long past, but it is in the cultural memory of the Welsh Language Society's crusade. A French philologist wrote a book not so long ago called *Deconloniser la France.* He attacked the attitude of the Paris sophisticate to the culture of, for instance, the Occitan whose language was one of the literary beauties of Europe when French was the means of communication of military barbarians like Simon de Montfort.

Morvan Lebesque, a brilliant journalist, taught himself Breton as a child in the face of bitter opposition at school. To the amazement of his teachers, his written French simultaneously won him school prizes. In a charming book *Comment Peut-On Etre Breton,* he wrote in the conclusion: 'I knew then why the recognition that I was Breton mattered. It mattered because it made me happy.' With a new 'enlightenment' taking place in Europe, minority languages are increasingly seen as precious and worthy of protection, and endangered species. It is really rather wonderful to live where there is still another language, older and richer than news-speak. Ecology is not only about physical pollution.

France, in a European *cordon sanitaire,* has abandoned her centralism and has come to appreciate the extraordinary richness of her regions, some of which were once kingdoms in their own right. Whatever latter-day Thatcherites may think, the nineteenth-century nation state is no longer viable in Europe. This makes the identity of the different groups and regions, which will constitute whatever new forms of government evolve, all the more precious and worthy of protection. There is a strong movement, a groundswell, taking place where old nations, like Wales and Brittany, seek to protect and reaffirm their identity in a European framework.

The present government of the United Kingdom is heavily centralist and certainly very English. Wales and Scotland have devolved executive government, but real authority is at Westminster. Moreover, the United Kingdom not being federal, neither Scotland nor Wales have regional parliamentary assemblies. This makes it all the more vital that English people who come to live in Wales should understand the fragility of a social scene already under threat from central government. Having lived in other countries, I think English culture has a grave deficiency, whether bred of superiority or insularity, I do not know. The English as a people are intellectually incurious. The exceptions to this rather bland statement make the generality more telling.

A country's physical beauty may carry a threat to its indigenous way of life. Visitors do not necessarily appreciate that an area of attractive landscape may also be the home of a unique civilisation. This fundamental dichotomy lies behind the ravages caused by mass tourism. The rush to the Spanish coast for the sun has destroyed what was once a strong, local community. This is not to say that such local communities should not change, many want to, but the shock of too sudden an introduction of alien values can be fatal. The same dichotomy is implicit in the relationship between rural depopulation and the inward penetration of outsiders establishing holiday and retirement homes.

My first childhood was in Australia, in the outback; my second in the United States; then I came to England, aged fourteen, and to all intents and purposes became very English. Since 1950, and until retirement, our working lives were spent in continental Europe, but our house in Wales has been our real home. It is said that Australians who become Europeanised suffer from an abiding sense of loss of roots. If this is true, it was perhaps the sentiment of certain European minorities, including the Welsh. In 1974 my book, *The Roots of Identity,* grew out of this type of terrain in which they flourish. Federal countries seldom have separatist movements; they flourish in highly-centralised bureaucracies. The Basque, the Breton and the Welsh movements were examined in the setting of contemporary European politics, but my early experience of life in north Wales after the war came before these later interests. An instinctive understanding at that time of the differences between Welsh and English attitudes provided the ground for detailed study. The national movements of the late nineteenth and twentieth centuries were started in the capital cities of what one could call the occupying powers. The Welsh who felt exiled from their own country staged the first National Eisteddfod since Elizabethan times on Primrose Hill in London. Under our present governmental structure, Welsh identity is in greater danger than the burgeoning regions of continental Europe. The role of the English incomer is therefore not a purely individual matter. He or she can hinder or abet the decline of what the editors of this book call 'Welshness'.

Capel-y-Ffin, by Suzanne Greenslade

BORDER
Gillian Clarke

It crumbles
where the land forgets its name
and I'm foreign in my own country.
Fallow, pasture, ploughland
ripped from the hill
beside a broken farm.

The word's exactness
slips from children's tongues.
Saints fade in the parishes.
Fields blur between the scar
of hedgerow and new road.
History forgets itself.

At the garage they're polite.
'Sorry love, no Welsh.'
At the shop I am slapped
by her hard 'What!'
They came for the beauty
but could not hear it speak.

'A DISSERVICE TO WELSH SCHOLARSHIP'
Pennar Davies

In my story Welshness was discovered rather than inherited. It is true that my father spoke what he called, without pride, 'Rhondda Welsh', but he never used it in our home except when another, perhaps more devoted, Welsh speaker called to have a chat with him. My mother came from a non-Welsh-speaking South Pembrokeshire family but spent her school years chiefly in the Welsh-speaking village of Hirwaun where her inability to speak Welsh made her something of an outsider.

My three sisters and I were brought up in the mining town of Aberpennar, more widely known as Mountain Ash, to speak English only, though we were sent in our early years to Ffrwd Welsh Baptist Chapel on the other side of the river Cynon. My father's father had been one of the founding members of this church, but my father was no chapel-goer. Brought up as a Welsh Calvinistic Methodist in the Rhondda, he had been alienated from religion by the excesses of the Evan Roberts revival coming on top of the strict Calvinistic devotion of his foster-parents.

We children were shepherded to and from Ffrwd Chapel by neighbours who lived on the opposite side of the street and took their own children there. The mother or the big sister would take us down to the main thoroughfare of the town and then over the bridge, that crossed the railway and the river, in the direction of the Town Hall. After crossing we would turn left and soon came to the old, humped, stone bridge over the canal, and passing St. Margaret's Church on our right walked to Ffrwd Chapel also on our right.

We went only to the morning service and the Sunday School in the afternoon. I do not remember any address to children in any language in the morning service. My sisters and I, with other children, sat in the body of the chapel not far from the pulpit. Some of the other children no doubt understood more than we did. Reading, prayer and sermon were meticulously, if mechanically, delivered by the tall and dignified preacher. I gradually came to the conclusion that he was the 'Iesu Grist' whose name he frequently uttered—an illogical inference which, I am told, is not uncommon among very young children.

The lady who taught the Sunday School class which I attended was motherly, warmhearted and conscientious. She used both languages and so I learnt little or no Welsh. Yet it was under her tuition that I learnt the Welsh alphabet and the pronunciation of Welsh words. She used one of those pictorial charts draped over a blackboard. I can hear her still saying 'Be kind', 'Be good' and 'Keep on trying'.

My impression is that she did more for me, in this regard, than did the teachers at my day school, although in other respects my debt to them is great indeed. I imagine that Dyffryn School was no worse, in respect of the teaching of Welsh, than schools in other areas in which Welsh speakers were menacingly outnumbered. One day, I happened to find an official time-table and saw that officially there were to be two lessons a week in Welsh. Even this meagre provision was largely ignored. In one year the teacher used the two periods to talk in Welsh with the handful of Welsh speakers among the pupils, telling the rest of us to read English books.

However, St. David's Day was not forgotten, and when I was about seven years of age I was required to learn a Welsh poem for recitation before an audience of children and parents. My eldest sister Jess had been presented in 1917 with a bound volume of *Cymru'r Plant* for the year 1916, and I set about learning a poem published in that magazine, namely 'Dydd Gŵyl Dewi Sant' by J. D. James. Without help I could not understand the words, but I think I got help from my father when he was on leave from the army. It seems, however, that I could recite the poem with unction. Fortunately, it was free from the war fever which afflicted even *Cymru'r Plant* in those days.

Despite my transference to a nearby English-language church, a Welsh loyalty began to grow in me. It was not fostered by my parents— except in a curious and unintended way by my father. He claimed that the Welsh were the bravest and best soldiers in the British Army and that they were often unfairly chosen by English officers to face the most dangerous tasks in the fighting. He often quoted some commander who, in some threatening situation, had cried out, 'Stick it, the Welsh!'—or rather the 'Welch' in the military spelling of the word.

When I entered the County School at Mountain Ash in 1922, the intake of Welsh-speaking and non-Welsh-speaking pupils was evenly balanced and so it was decided to separate the A class and the B class on grounds not of ability, as was the custom, but of language. As a non-Welsh-speaker I found myself in the A stream where the Welsh teacher was Miss Ethel James. I liked Welsh as a subject but did not dream of learning to speak it. I made progress and after three years or so the headmaster, a valiant Welshman named W. U. Williams, wanted to transfer me to the Welsh-speaking stream. I resisted out of regard for Miss James and was allowed to stay in her class. When, after receiving my 'Senior' Certificate, I chose to do Latin, Welsh and English for the

41

'Higher' Certificate, I found myself in a very small class taught splendidly by Miss John. But speaking Welsh freely and naturally was far beyond my capacity.

Entering the University College, Cardiff, in 1929, I kept my three subjects, adding to them a modicum of Greek. I kept Welsh to the 'Final' stage and took Latin and English further to the Honours stage. I still could not speak Welsh and was too shy to venture. For this sin of omission I was severely and publicly reprimanded by the outstanding Welsh scholar Griffith John Williams, who said—in English—that my failure to speak Welsh was 'a disservice to Welsh scholarship'. I could read it and write it as well as I could read and write English, but did not venture to converse in it until I let myself go in the gentle and warmhearted company of a new friend, Gwyn (John Gwynedd) Griffiths, as we paddled a boat on the river Cherwell at Oxford in the year 1935.

In 1943 I married Rosemarie Wolff, a refugee from Nazi Germany. Her native language was German, but she had learnt English at school and spoke it extremely well. She had become a nurse at a hospital in Oxford. After our marriage (in a service at Oxford conducted by a German pastor), she learnt Welsh very quickly and ever since has been able to converse in it most acceptably. We have five children, a daughter and four sons, and Welsh is their first language. The eldest son is a lecturer in the Welsh Department of one of our University Colleges. One of his brothers operates in a Welsh translating agency. The youngest helps to manage a bookshop in which the selling of Welsh books has pride of place. My daughter teaches, and is active in Welsh-speaking circles in a border region. The other son works in a department store, and Welsh-speaking customers like to turn to him and shop in Welsh. I have two grandsons, a ten-year-old who is Welsh-speaking and a baby whose first words I expect to be Welsh.

Writing in Welsh, I feel that I am writing not for a market but for a community. By this I mean that the profit motive cannot be a dominant one in the commitment of a Welsh-language writer. There is no such thing as a full-time author in the Welsh language—except in the case of an occasional old-age pensioner. Like almost every other Welsh author I have had to write in my spare time. We have a small number of journalists, of course, who live partly by their writing and partly by serving their firms in other ways; but, on the whole, literary work in the Welsh language is a labour of love. Of course, every Welsh language writer hopes for recognition as do writers in all other languages, but his dominant interest is cultural and not financial.

The Welsh-language writer's reward is not 'success' measured in monetary terms, but the quiet joy of knowing that he is contributing to the ongoing cultural life of a national community which, for centuries, has been linguistically persecuted, his language having been deprived of official status and social prestige.

Perhaps I should add my thanks to those who have given me a measure of inspiration and encouragement. I have already mentioned Miss James and Miss John in my secondary school and the headmaster himself who, I remember, in the school's annual assembly for teachers, pupils and parents, quoted from a patriotic Welsh poem which I had contributed to the school magazine. I honour also my parents who, although they had not brought me up to speak Welsh, did not discourage me from seeking to recover my Welsh identity and became increasingly sympathetic and helpful.

During my time at the University College, Cardiff, I attended lectures by W. J. Gruffydd, Griffith John Williams and T. J. Morgan and so came to appreciate Welsh scholarship and explore the treasures of Welsh literature; but English became my chief subject. Some of my research work on John Bale was published by the Oxford Bibliographical Society but I have made no attempt to publish my long doctoral dissertation on the Jacobean dramatist and translator George Chapman. This is because my main field of interest had changed and I sought to serve in the Christian ministry. I also found myself sharing the interests of *Cylch Cadwgan*, the Cadwgan Circle, a group of young and aspiring Welsh writers and patriots. We met at 'Cadwgan', the Rhondda home of Käthe Bosse-Griffiths and her husband J. Gwyn Griffiths. D. R. Griffiths, his brother, and Rhydwen Williams are accounted members of the group.

The lesson would seem to be 'Nothing venture, nothing win'. In a way *Cymraeg* is not my first language. It is the medium of most of my literary work. I write in Welsh, as I have said, not for a market but for a community. This is broadly true of the world's great ancient literatures and of living literatures which, like literature in the Welsh language, have enduring roots in the past. Yet the Welsh language is splendidly adaptable and lends itself readily to modern requirments. To lose it would be to impoverish the life of mankind.

IN JOHN JONES COUNTRY
Meic Stephens

If it is possible to be Welsh without speaking the language, as I believe it is, then I am no more Welsh today, at the age of fifty-one, having learned the language, than I was when, as a young man of seventeen, I spoke only English. For the first third of my life I knew scarcely any Welsh and yet, from the moment I began to think about such matters, I was always quite sure not only that I *was* Welsh, but that even if I were to learn the language, I could hardly be *more* Welsh than I already was. There has been nothing yet in the subsequent two-thirds of my life that has persuaded me to think otherwise.

To make the point clearer, I must set down some facts. First of all, I consider myself Welsh because I was born in Wales—at Treforest, near Pontypridd in Glamorgan, and it was there that I grew up during the 1940s. Our house was just across the railway and a field from the School of Mines, the old home of Francis Crawshay, the local iron-master, that I am still not used to calling the Polytechnic of Wales. We belonged, of course, to the working-class (there was only one class in Treforest), but we were not poor and there was nothing rough about us. Both my father and my grandfather were skilled men with steady jobs in the electricity industry and, except for the long summer of 1926, had never been unemployed. My father worked all his life, from tea boy to turbine driver, in the power station at Upper Boat, a few miles down the valley, and my grandfather was a cable-man with the Pontypridd Urban District Council. Each brought home a decent wage, so that neither my mother nor my grandmother had to go out to work, like some women in Meadow Street, although they were kept busy at home, cooking, washing and mending. Our house had only six small rooms but it was clean, warm and comfortable, and we lived in it, mostly in the kitchen, cheerfully enough. There was always enough to eat, even when food was rationed, we were well-clothed my brother and I, and my parents never failed to pay their way; we were, in short, a *tidy* family, and we boys were not allowed to forget it. Our neighbours, too, were as 'ordinary' in the Raymond Williams sense as ourselves—hard-working, law-abiding, warm-hearted, long-suffering—and whatever tastes I may have since acquired, it is among such people that I still feel most at home.

Secondly, I am Welsh because my parents were Welsh, and that, too, has always been good enough for me. My father had been brought up as a policeman's son at Heolgerrig in Merthyr Tydfil and later at

Rhydfelen, on the other side of the Taff from Treforest, near where the Welsh comprehensive school stands today. Of the Welsh language he had only a smattering, about enough to speak to a dog, but he was well enough disposed towards it and felt its lack keenly. His mother's people, the Lloyds, were from the hills of Radnorshire, where they had practised their skills as bone-setters for generations. Their graves are in such quiet places as Glascwm and Llansanffraid-yn-Elfael, Huntington and Michaelchurch-on-Arrow. Perhaps my most remarkable kinsman was the John Lloyd, known in folk tradition as Silver John, who was murdered near New Radnor in about the year 1814. He, too, was a charmer and was killed, by persons unknown, for the silver baubles sewn on his coat which he took as payment for his remedies. In our own time the most distinguished Lloyd was Evan Lloyd, a surgeon at Guy's Hospital in London, and there is another who is a chiropractor in Cardiff. Having traced the lineage of these Lloyds to the mid-eighteenth century, in Elfael and Maelienydd, I am satisfied that the family was indigenous to Radnorshire and that my father was, in the genealogical sense, Welsh. In my more omphalosceptic moments, such as this, I like to fancy that from these border people, with whose hardy breed I feel a special affinity, I inherited not only my long legs and fair complexion, but something else besides, although since I know them only from photographs and hearsay, I cannot be sure as to what that might be. I feel it most while reading Kilvert's Diary (in which several Lloyds are mentioned) and whenever I walk the country between Builth and Hay.

Of my mother's provenance I am less certain. I know that she was born in Treforest, in the very street we lived and she still lives in, and that by temperament and outlook she is as Welsh as the rest of us. She, too, has only a passing acquaintance with the language, singing hymns and reading from the Welsh Bible without understanding more than a few words, but because I have never looked into the origins of her parents, my Nan and Grampa, who lived with us, I cannot swank a family tree on the distaff side. All I know about my grandmother is that she was from Bedwellty in the Sirhowy valley and that her father, too, had been a policeman. That she was Welsh was taken for granted because she was easily recognisable as one of us and perhaps, in her Silurian way, she was the most Welsh of us all. The only difference was that, whereas we went to chapel, she claimed to belong to the Church. As I do not recall her ever attending church, I think her allegiance (like that of voting Tory) must have been a deferential habit she had picked up while in the service of the Powell family, the Cardiff shipowners, who had employed her as a girl.

'Matilda's off to church', my grandfather used to say whenever she tried to put on airs, and the name by which she had been known as a parlour-maid would always make her laugh and drop the silly pretence.

It was in Cardiff that she and my grandfather had first met, one wet afternoon in 1905. On an errand to the shops for her mistress, she was sheltering from a thundery downpour in the entrance of the Royal Arcade when, against her better judgement, as she always put it, she found herself talking to a young man who had jumped out of a waterlogged trench in St. Mary's Street. It was literally *un coup de foudre*. She fell, it seems, for his jaunty bowler and the red carnation in the lapel of his muddy jacket. By the time the sky had cleared they had arranged to meet again on her next half-day and by the end of the year they were married and settled in Treforest. I digress if only to suggest how much a matter of the merest chance—in my case a shower of rain—one's genetic inheritance can be.

Turning now to my grandfather, I have to make an exception to my previous assertion that everyone in our family was Welsh. As a matter of fact, my grandfather was English—a Londoner from King's Cross, who had come to Cardiff at the age of twenty-five to work under contract on a scheme for the electrification of the city's trams. Cardiff at the time was in its heyday as a coal port and he was among the many thousands who were moving into south-east Wales in search of work. Now it might be thought that, with an English grandfather, our household and my boyhood would have been that much the less Welsh, but it turned out not to be so. He had been living in Wales, remember, for some thirty years by the time I was born. Indeed, it seems that he had gone back to London only for brief visits, virtually losing touch with his family until contact between them had dwindled to a card at Christmas and little more. It is not often that I think of them, but I must have relatives in England, second cousins by now, and I do not even know their names. Who was it said that the Welsh and English are, like Christmas cake and Christmas pudding, made of much the same ingredients but cooked in different ways? Be that as it may, it seemed to me as a boy that my grandfather had become so like the people amongst whom he had settled that there was nothing much to distinguish him from the rest of us. Or perhaps, at that time and in that place, the proletariat had other, more compelling things on its mind, so that such considerations had little relevance to our lives and were therefore seldom remarked upon.

It was only as I began to grow up, and my imagination to be stirred, that it gradually dawned on me that there *was* something different about my grandfather, after all. This slight incongruity (it was hardly more

46

than that) had to do with the way in which he used the English language. We all spoke English with a Welsh accent, of course, and he had picked up our dialect during the long years of his assimilation. But from time to time, especially when excited, he would revert to the broader vowels of his London youth, often with startling effect. His register on these occasions would be quite different from ours and he would use expressions that were not in our idiom. One of his favourite exclamations, for example, was 'Godfrey and Daniel, blast-furnace manufacturers'. Sometimes he would remember even more vivid phrases—some rhyming slang, perhaps, or the patter of the music-hall—that seemed to me to have an exotic charm of their own, as if they belonged to another world. And so it was, as I pricked up my ears to the nuances of the English language, that I came not only to recognise my grandfather's otherness, but also to see the rest of the family, and myself, in a new light.

It was a slow, subtle, imperceptible process, part of the complexity of late adolescence, and I am not absolutely certain that I am describing it now, in retrospect, in sufficient detail or with complete accuracy. To make matters even more complicated, there was a difference between the characters of my grandfather and my father that was to prove crucial as far as I was concerned. My father was a quiet, reflective, cautious man who liked his own company best, having a natural reserve that may have been inherited from his Radnorshire forebears. Whereas he was thrifty, conscientious, well-mannered and teetotal, my grandfather—'a proper rodney' in my grandmother's mysterious phrase—was talkative, gregarious, devil-may-care and fond of his pint. Unlike my father, who worked shifts and was often not at home in the evenings and at weekends, the older man kept more regular hours and was usually to be found about the house, especially during his retirement in the years just after the war, so that I spent a good deal of time in his company as a child. He would entertain me with word-games and tunes on his tin whistle, and tell me stories about three characters named Ampam, Volto and Watty, and take me for walks up the Barry mountain, the wooded hill behind Treforest, where I learned from him the names of birds and butterflies and flowers. One summer afternoon, I remember, we walked through Ton-teg and Efailisaf to the summit of the Garth and from the tumulus there I saw, as if by revelation, the valleys of Glamorgan winding smokily to the north, the Beacons in the far distance, and below us, Cardiff shimmering in the heat, and beyond, the Channel and the hazy hills of Somerset. I think that must have been the day when a map started to form in my mind that I have carried about with me ever since,

Penrhiwceiber Workmen's Hall & Institute, by David Bailey

and at that spot, to which I often return, I never fail to feel the primaeval tug, that sense of belonging to a particular place, which is at the root of patriotism.

Between the temperaments of my father and my grandfather there was, then, a difference, an antipathy perhaps, that the growing boy could not but perceive. This curious reversal of the usual stereotypes—the phlegmatic, fastidious, rather gentlemanly Welshman and the excitable, easy-going extrovert Englishman—might have had little enough effect on me if the paradox had ended there. But there was this difference, too: whereas my father's work left him time only for the most mundane things, my grandfather encouraged me to listen to the wireless and talked to me about whatever happened to be the serious news of the day. He had lived through the Boer Wars, two world wars and the Depression in the years between, so he had a lot to reminisce about. Among his heroes were Keir Hardie and Aneurin Bevan (with a nod in the direction of Lloyd George), and he spoke of the Tonypandy Riots and the Senghennydd Explosion as if they had happened only the other day. On the subject of Tonypandy he was particularly adamant, summing up the question of whether or not Churchill had sent the troops with the verdict that 'Even if he didn't, he did', and he was among those who swore to having seen a glow in the sky above Senghennydd, just over Mynydd Meio from Treforest, on the night *before* the disaster at the Universal Colliery. It was this talk about local history, however highly coloured, that fascinated me. Soon I was hearing about some of the famous people who had been associated with the district in which we lived. There was, for instance, the eccentric Dr William Price—neo-druid, Chartist and cremationist—who had paraded through the streets of Treforest in his fox-skin hat and with burning torch in hand, and whose memorial is the crematorium at Glyn-taf, 'across the river' as we used to say, as if the Taff were the Styx. The village was rich in industrial archaeology: we had a canal, feeders, foundries and sidings, all derelict, and splendid places for boys to play, that were among the oldest in Wales. Nearby were the Brown Lenox chainworks, and in Cil-haul, at the bottom of our street beyond the Bute embankment, lay the Crawshays' old tinplate works, around which Treforest had originally grown. About a mile up the valley, the story of the Old Bridge was waiting to be told and I remember being taken to see, in Ynys Angharad Park, the monument to the composers of *Hen Wlad fy Nhadau*. In this way I was introduced to what my grandfather sometimes called 'John Jones's country': that small part of Wales—industrial, English-speaking but nonetheless Welsh— which he knew and evidently wanted to share with me.

49

I wish it were possible for me to go on to relate how I was helped towards a better understanding of things Welsh by my experiences in chapel and school, but alas, that was not to be. At Libanus, the Baptist chapel I attended as a boy, the hymns and sermons were usually in Welsh and I dimly recall seeing some of the elders reading a denominational newspaper that must have been *Seren Gomer*, but the language of the congregation was otherwise English. What I remember most about chapel are the interminable rehearsals for the annual singing-festival and the squabbling among the members. It was a huge relief when, in my fifteenth year, I was given to understand that I need not go to Sunday School or the Band of Hope unless I wanted to, and soon afterwards I stopped going altogether. To this day I find it difficult to sit through a Welsh chapel service without suffering again the tedium of those Sundays at Libanus. I was no more fortunate as a pupil at the Pontypridd Boys' Grammar School, where I went in 1949, having come second in my year at the entrance examination (I was never to reach those heights again). There I found Welsh history to be exclusively concerned with the luminaries of the Methodist Revival and I dropped Welsh in favour of French, as the brighter boys were encouraged to do, at the first opportunity. Whereas I was taught English and French by excellent teachers whom I recall with gratitude, I found the learning of Welsh a dreadful fatigue, something of which is reflected in my poem 'Elegy for Mr Lewis (Welsh)'. In three years I managed only to count up to twenty and to recite some simple rhymes. It was only on St. David's Day, at the school eisteddfod, that Welsh was used in the assembly hall and even then, for me, the experience of hearing it was not unlike that of singing hymns in chapel. No, I cannot say that either school or chapel did much to nurture in me the growing sense of being Welsh, and there was no other agent that might have done so. Some of our neighbours belonged to choirs or amateur dramatic societies, but the only entertainment outside the home for our family was the local cinema, where we never saw ourselves.

The likelihood is that, if it had not been for my grandfather, things might have remained thus, and so to him—the one identifiable counter-influence upon me at this time—I must now return. If I am mistaken and he had no deliberate intention of interesting me in Wales, I am ready to admit the possibility, but if that was indeed the case, then I find myself at a loss to explain (unless this, too, was quite fortuitous) why it was, on my seventeenth birthday in 1955, my grandfather gave me the *Selected Poems of Idris Davies*, inscribing it neatly in his elegant hand. I still have that book and whenever I take it down it serves as well as any madeleine to remind me of the excitement, almost feverish in intensity, with which I first read about the place and people that I was quick to recognise as my own. Oh, I know now how easy it is to fall under the spell of poetry that is full of familiar place-names and homely sentiment and meant to win the reader over to its particular point of view, but I responded then—it was not unlike falling in love for the first time—with a candour and delight about which I still do not feel any embarrassment and which I wish, sometimes, it were possible to recapture and enjoy again.

It proved to be a decisive experience, that reading of Idris Davies in the summer of 1955, and thereafter my course was irrevocably set. Already a bookish lad, a real Hoggart boy, I turned from reading Greek and Nordic mythology to working my way through the Local Authors section of the Pontypridd Public Library. Soon, within the year, I had read Jack Jones, Dylan Thomas, Caradoc Evans, Glyn Jones, Gwyn Thomas, Rhys Davies, Gwyn Jones, Alun Lewis, and many another Welsh author whose work was to be found on those dusty, marvellously jumbled shelves. In this I was encouraged by the young woman who lived next door to us: an assistant in the library, she would reserve books of Welsh interest for me and let me borrow more than the rules allowed. As I read, I began to realize that there were places like Treforest in other parts of Wales, and I resolved to set out and see them with my own eyes as often as I could. I began by taking the bus up the Rhondda Valleys (which seemed to me the quintessential Wales), and then to Aberdare, Merthyr, Rhymney and Ebbw Vale, and over the Beacons to Brecon and beyond. In some of these places I had relatives and, on the pretext of visiting them, I would spend my Saturdays and holidays walking the streets, wandering on the hills above the towns and talking to anyone I met on the way. I even got as far as Cardiff, in the 1950s a day's excursion from the valleys, and tasted the pleasures of a city for which I have ever since felt a real affection.

Thus I began to discover for myself the history, literature, topography and people of a Wales wider than the one I had known up to then. Looking back—not without a feeling of 'Say, could that lad be I?'—I am aware that for those who take the language to be the *sine qua non* of Welsh nationality, my Wales may not have been recognisable as Welsh at all, and that the experience I have described might well be discounted. Such a view fills me with dismay, for it seems to deny or ignore the reality of how the people of Wales, or the greater part of them, have lived during the twentieth century, but it does not leave me entirely cast down. Wales is a small country and the Welsh, even at three million, are a small people, yet still not so small that they do not have to rely on diversity for

51

whatever unity they might, on occasion, wish to claim. We come to see ourselves as Welsh, and to make our commitment to Wales, for different reasons and in different ways, and there seems to be little point in falling out over it. Perhaps, instead, we should try now to accept the differences and go on to explore what we have in common and what we might yet make of it.

As for myself, I have known for many years what I want for Wales. Just after my grandfather's retirement in 1945, the Electrical Trades Union presented him with a gold medallion, 'for services rendered'. I remember the pride with which he first showed it to me, drawing my attention to the union's motto inscribed upon it: 'Light and Liberty'. Today that medallion is one of my most precious things and, more and more in recent years, whenever I hear the knives of dogma being sharpened, I have found myself contemplating the meaning of those words. Yes, Light and Liberty.

ELEGY FOR MR. LEWIS (Welsh)
Meic Stephens

Sir, I was your pupil for five years
but you taught me nothing, except to recite
that verse about a little woman who sold black sweets,
and how to count up to ten. Without a doubt
you must have been the worst teacher in our school.

You won't remember me. I was the boy, no
duffer, who sat anonymous through your dreadful classes
and was never asked a question, but who still
recalls the famous sarcasm and the ferocious stick
by which a generation came to fear you.

I wonder what made you such a monster:
was it, perhaps, some private, ineffable grief
that you took out on us? No, I don't mean cancer
nor your flighty wife who ran away with an accountant,
but the more malignant knowledge that, for us,

Welsh seemed as obsolete as Etruscan
that only farmers and a few fanatics spoke.
After all, what did Glyndŵr or Pantycelyn have
to say to us whose heroes were alive and relevant?
We cheered our own in cinema and stadium.

It's no secret that you failed at the job;
but why, so often from my desk in the back row, did
I catch you staring across the valleys, tears
in your eyes, at the shining hill above Eglwys Ilan?
Old bully, ranting forever in my memory,

you've been dead these twenty years. Well,
I speak and love the language now, no thanks to you;
so please allow me, late as usual but not far wrong,
to raise my hand for once and make this reply:
Cymro, I know what drove you to despair.

OPEN SECRETS
Emyr Humphreys

Every landscape treasures its secrets. Children stumble across them without any immediate need to put them into words. Beyond the narrow belt of trees, above the sheep droppings and the clumps of gorse and limestone outcrops, there is a cave on the hillside that is equally suitable for prehistoric man, bandits, Indians, and schoolboys smoking their first cigarette. The school textbook says that in one 'chamber' of the cave fifteen skeletons were found closely packed together in a crouched position. A delectable, mute, mystery. And on top of the hill, the man-made tumulus is named Y Gop, where local legend persists in saying Boadicea is buried. A long way from home. What language did she speak? Dig our soil and you find eloquent oval cups, oak overlaid with gold, and thin breastplates for horses embossed and worked by hands that knew how to speak without words. The views from the hilltop are enticing, intoxicating. North-east lies the Wirral, where the Green Knight hides, mixing Celtic legends with Middle-English poetry. Westwards the white strength of Gwynedd, and the mountains rising like ramparts to touch the setting sun. From every point of the compass this unique landscape hides treasure trove. Even the impassive vastness of the level sea conceals sunken cities with secret histories, myths and legends.

To each mystery there must be a key: but the key of keys is the original language which hallows every hill and valley, every farm and every field with its own revered name. I must learn it and the more difficult it is the better. Hidden treasures like pearls and lost souls need to have their price. Cromlechs and chronicles, Celtic crosses and Roman mines, castles and chapels, wells, caves, coalmines and churches, ruined abbeys and choirs, 'the woods, waters, meadows, combes, vales/ All the air things wear that build this world of Wales'.

In the public library in the Town Hall of Rhyl, where the patient books lie sheltered from the cacophanous uproar of Pleasureland and the variegated mechanical marvels of the Marine Lake, I discover to my amazed delight that Gerard Manley Hopkins lived in Tremeirchion, just over the hill from our village, and learnt Welsh. What else could a poet do? What a claim we had on the world! What a birthright! This 'man in black', wrestling in secret with our *cynghanedd*, was to have a revolutionary effect on the making of poetry in an English language that was stretching itself to bestride the globe like a commercial Colossus.

54

We had and we have our own manifest destiny. T. S. Eliot used to refer to the poetic process having the fortunate by-product of purifying the language of the tribe. Others have related the pollution of 'admass' to visible deterioration in the environment. We all have our responsibilities. In Wales this must involve the realisation that it is out of our language —our ancient language—that this landscape is best celebrated and renewed, the human environment cleansed, enriched, and renewed: the tidal wave of corrosive pollution stemmed. Take a year, take a lifetime, to hammer out a defence from this unique song that is *Cymraeg*.

CHOOSING WALES
Raymond Garlick

In a very real sense it was the health of my great-aunt Kate in the early years of the century which was ultimately responsible for the fact that Wales has been my home for most of the past fifty years. As was the way then, she was told by her doctor that some condition from which she suffered could be alleviated by living on the coast of Gwynedd. I wonder whether medical practitioners still issue such migratory advice. At all events she took it and settled, well before the 1914-18 war, at Degannwy on the estuary of the Conwy. I don't know what she suffered from, but the prescription, presumably, worked as she was still flourishing there in the early 1930s. As a small child I remember her well, in her imposing black-and-white house with its large conservatory and grapevine laden with huge bunches of purple-bloomed fruit. Be-toqued and pearled, stately, bright-eyed, and slightly gaga, there was attached to her something of the aura associated with Mrs. Williams in Dylan Thomas's story 'The Peaches', for she too was a mayoress. Her husband, my great-uncle Charles Whitmill, controller of the LMS Railway between Chester and Holyhead, became mayor of Conwy in the mid-1930s, and there was an imposing portrait of him in full mayoral fig of scarlet, lace and budge.

This clearly implies a commitment to the country of their adoption, and their daughter (though English-born) certainly thought of herself as a Welshwoman, had some knowledge of Welsh, and became a Jones by marriage. My father's favourite cousin and contemporary, she was conveniently packaged as an honorary aunt, and in her busy household I spent the first years of the 1939-1945 war. She and her warmly-eccentric husband, a master baker and confectioner, were in business in Degannwy—employing a staff of some half-dozen, all of whom were Welsh speakers—and it was there that I acquired my first Welsh phrase, *Cymru am byth* (which appeared on tins of toffee on sale in the shop), to be followed by many more.

This was not, however, my first Welsh word, which had been acquired many years earlier. Encouraged, no doubt, by the amelioration in my great-aunt's health, my grandparents had followed her example upon retiring from a modest business in London, and they too settled in Degannwy in 1930. In consequence, throughout the ensuing decade their house became a base for family holidays. The main stage of these, of course, was the Degannwy shore—where we rented a green-painted wooden beach-hut—and to reach this, then as now, it was necessary to cross the railway level-crossing. This in itself was a major attraction of Degannwy for a small boy. Ideally one hoped to reach the level-crossing just as the signalman leaned out of the window of his box, rang the bell, and began turning the great wheel—like the steering-wheel of a ship—that closed the gates, and thus gave a close-up view of the train steaming past. It also gave time to read the warning notice, in raised letters on a metal plate, which began with the word *Rhybudd*. I never heard the word spoken, and pronounced it privately to myself as though it was an English word, knowing no better at the time. This was one of the very few Welsh words to be seen in public in those days. Though it was still possible to encounter elderly Welsh monoglots in rural Gwynedd, and Welsh was quite widely used in the Llandudno area, apart from chapel notice-boards it was visually arcane. The fairly widespread visibility of Welsh today is quite recent, and a consequence of *Cymdeithas yr Iaith*[1] campaigns.

My great-aunt Kate's health—or rather an unknown doctor's advice—at a period when I did not even exist, thus set in motion a whole chain of reactions which resulted in annual holidays in Degannwy, and my being sent there to school at the outbreak of the 1939 war. The school in question (now headed by a past-pupil of mine) was the John Bright County School in Llandudno—civilized, anarchic, offering superb teaching, and still very Welsh. Most of its excellent and characterful staff were graduates of the University of Wales, and—perhaps prompted by a visit of Principal Sir Emrys Evans to the school's speech day—it

[1] The Welsh Language Society

seemed natural to want to go on to University College, Bangor, as I did in 1944.

Here such scholars as Sir John Edward Lloyd and Sir Ifor Williams were still to be encountered in corridor and library, and I was taught philosophy by Professor Hywel D. Lewis and Welsh history by Dr. R. T. Jenkins. Among fellow-students at Bangor at the time were Islwyn Ffowc Elis, Meredydd Evans, Tom Ellis, and, latterly, Emyr Humphreys (already with a first novel to his name). I made the acquaintance of such distinguished Welshmen as Dr. Thomas Parry, Alun Llywelyn-Williams, Dr. Pennar Davies, Professor J. E. Daniel, Professor T. Jones Pierce. To an English student Bangor, at that time, seemed intensely and naturally Welsh and Welsh-speaking, and I certainly wanted to be a part of this to the extent that it was possible.

Identity is formed not only by a predisposition in favour of certain things but also by antipathy to others. Though London suburbia held me for considerably longer than the period said to be required by the Jesuits to make a child their own—in fact for the first thirteen years of my life, so that I shall always be an Englishman—for as far back as I can remember I had a strong antipathy to it. To begin with it was simply so vast and sprawling and raw and characterless. Even then there was an awareness of fields, hedges, farms, woods, being devoured by the brash, new, pink housing-estates. By the beginning of adolescence there was an obscure consciousness of some of the suburban values of the late 1930s— British chauvinism, Philistinism, xenophobia, petty snobbery, Protestant sectarianism, and overall an ineffable smugness and complacency—and an inarticulate hostility to them. The annual exploration of the Creuddyn peninsula and the serene valley of the Conwy, and the later experiences as schoolboy and undergraduate, offered welcome alternatives to some of this. The visual splendour of north-western Gwynedd and Eryri, the mountains and lakes and seashore, was the point of departure for a wonder which swept me as a child, and is undiminished to this day. Yet from the beginning there was an awareness that it was not only the magnificence of the landscape which moved and attracted, but its otherness—its Welshness, its place-names, its history, its daily language, its life and values so far as these could be glimpsed.

The full and final formulation of identity is reached by acts of choice and will. The process of legal naturalization in states which provide for it is a recognition of this fact. Though there is no formal procedure by which one becomes a citizen of Wales, the consequences of such a commitment are much the same: a responsibility towards the culture and language of the adopted country (especially if one has children to educate and bring up), a duty to defend it, and an obligation to cast one's vote in general and local elections in what one judges to be its best interests. The event which at the time seemed to precipitate this commitment for me was moving to south Pembrokeshire in 1949 to take up my first teaching appointment. It was a fine school, and I was happy in it. South Pembrokeshire is, of course, a beautiful part of Wales with a distinctive character and history, but—going there from the cottage on the 800' contour on Moel Faban, above the Ogwen valley, which had been my home for the previous two years—I was largely blind to this. Moreover, it was an enclave where the Welsh language had been absent for many centuries, and the corrupted Welsh or wholly English place-names grated on my ear. The contrast with Gwynedd was profound, and to this and what it embodied I now consciously committed myself—the real Wales as it seemed. Yet, paradoxically, it was while based in south Pembrokeshire that—as the young editor of the only Anglo-Welsh periodical then in existence—I became acquainted with (and published) Saunders Lewis, and it was there too that my friendships with D. J. Williams, Waldo Williams and R. S. Thomas began.

Gradually over the years, as I moved about Wales and saw its variety—and saw it too from the perspective of seven years' residence on the Continent in another small European country, I came to realize how naïve and provincial my earlier attitudes had been. To fragment Wales by exclusive enthusiasm for one particular *bro* is—in the native-born—parochialism, and for the incomer mere settler satisfaction: it is not at all the same thing as identifying with Wales. Choosing Wales involves choosing its diversity, its plurality, Gwynedd and south Pembrokeshire, Carmarthen and Cardiff, the industrial valleys of Gwent and Glamorgan as well as those of Eryri, Welsh-language and Anglo-Welsh cultures (for to ignore the latter is to be ignorant of a long dimension of Wales). This is something that many Welsh people have still to see clearly, and choosing Wales involves being clear-sighted about its weaknesses too—of which this very tendency to fragmentation is one. Like that of any other country ancient in origins but living in the last decade of the twentieth century, the identity of Wales is rich and complex. Those who seek to identify with it, to commit themselves to it, must grow into this complexity and discover their own place there.

'MODD I FYW'
Carl Clowes

The rag-and-bone man came once a week—a reassuring sound as the clip-clop of horses' hooves on the sets heralded our early attempts at recycling; the *tŷ bach* at the bottom of the yard and the washing hung out across the backs of the small, terraced houses—none were unusual experiences for many born in Wales in the 1940s. My childhood memories, however, relate to Manchester, a cosmopolitan city which had attracted many sons and daughters of rural Britain and beyond over the decades.

The evidence of migration was all around—immediate neighbours were of Irish and Scottish extraction. I attended a primary school run by two delightful Irish ladies. New Year's Eve was celebrated with as much enthusiasm as Christmas. Within a stone's throw was a strong Jewish community—a true community within the city. Beyond, the childhood home of Lloyd George and the several Welsh chapels frequented by Welsh exiles, my mother amongst them.

I went to chapel with my mother occasionally, very occasionally, not understanding most of the happenings. I sensed she wanted me to go and I responded from time to time, notwithstanding the relative futility of the experience.

My mother, born in Llanberis in Gwynedd, left school at 14. After a short period in London, she met her husband in Caernarfon whilst working in a small clothes shop. The owner of the shop was an early entrepreneur from Manchester! His brother worked alongside him for a while and was to become my father.

It wasn't long before mother was attracted to Manchester—be it fame or fortune, or was the grass really greener? I'll never know. My father took an apprenticeship as a joiner in Manchester and worked solidly as a skilled craftsman in just two companies all his working life—a small family company and, when that went to the wall, a 'multi-national' within bike- and later moped-distance.

Despite my mother's visits to chapel for her Welsh sustenance, the Welsh language in the home was taboo. Father's parents were stern and Welsh had no place. Mother's early attempts to introduce the language were thwarted. Family provocation created a self-embarrassment difficult to counter, not surprisingly in the relative isolation of the big city. That atmosphere in the home was never to change and the language never gained the credence it might have had in a more enlightened (and educated?) home.

By now one can look back at that family response and place it in perspective. As for so many, the language represented a threat—a threat based on ignorance. This ignorance could only have resulted as a consequence of the failure of the education system in England to recognise the plurality of culture within these islands, even at that time. Sadly, little has changed.

For every young child, *nain* (grandmother) has a particular significance. I was no exception and from the age of six I visited my mother's home in Llanberis annually, usually for the summer holiday. For a few special weeks each year Newton Street became the centre of my world. The trips to the corner shop, the bakehouse and paper shop, usually by myself, all left their impression. The sense of community was unmistakeable. So too was the smell—the smell of damp slate in the 'backs' of Llanberis—a small price to pay for the freedom of walking miles in and around this most beautiful part of Eryri—an area I came to know well and to love.

Llanberis in the 1950s was essentially a monoglot community. English had its place in the tourist industry but, in every other area of community and social life, Welsh was paramount. The predominance of Welsh added to the totality of my experience. For the first time I played with children whose only language was Welsh. With the help of *nain*, I learned to count in Welsh—up to 100!—and '*Gee Ceffyl Bach*' and the odd proverb became familiar territory.

I can only assume *nain* enjoyed my presence. I have vivid memories of provoking and teasing all day long, although there must have been times when loneliness in the home hit hard. She lost her husband aged 47. He had worked as a quarryman at Dinorwig nearby and succumbed to sarcoidosis, a close relative of tuberculosis, one of the all too frequent consequences of the industry. Of the seven children she had borne, only two had survived to adulthood, my mother, Mary Gwyneth, and her sister Eluned. After marrying, sister Eluned lived in nearby Allt Goch in Llanberis. That is, she did until she and her family came to live with us in Manchester.

Another family in exile. For me however this was to prove good news. The little terraced house could hardly accommodate the new arrivals, but now Welsh was to be heard at home for the first time. The family moved after several months but were still within walking distance, and the social and cultural stimulus remained.

My mother and father were two very different personalities—father undoubtedly inherited the protestant work ethic—worked hard, saved and lived safely; my mother, on the other hand, put great store on a good education, leading to a professional career and the potential for escape from relative poverty. Both were typical of their period in many ways, but both also reflected a totally different culture.

Not surprisingly, I have inherited some of the characteristics of both! At the age of fourteen, when visiting Llanberis with my mother, one of the great houses of the area was being sold by the RAF. Used as an officers' mess during the Second World War, Glyn Padarn failed to reach the asking price at auction. To my mother and myself it presented a remarkable opportunity, and without any further ado we sought details from RAF Burtonwood, near Warrington in Lancashire, catching the train and bus from Manchester to seek the necessary information. £1200 for a mansion! The sum seems incredible today. For my father the experience of buying it proved an agonising one. Never having been in debt and never having owned his own home, how could he consider spending all his savings and more on the property? The entrepreneurial enthusiasm of myself and my mother won the battle. We bought Glyn Padarn and my mother ran it as a guest house during the summer. On the other hand, my father's reluctance to venture and to complete the commitment ensured that he remained rooted to his nine-to-five existence in Manchester.

Commuting every weekend for my father became the norm. For myself, holidays were spent in Wales whilst term-time was spent in Manchester. Having won a precious entrance scholarship to Bury School, a fee-paying school to the north of Manchester, to relinquish the same would have been unthinkable to mother.

There was a touch of irony in my mother finding her way back to Glyn Padarn. Her family had been brought up in the lodge belonging to the house and her father raised in the quarrymen's cottages, now demolished, just a stone's throw above the house in Pen-y-Gilfach.

For me, Wales was now well and truly my home. At fourteen years of age I could say that I had never felt a part of the conurbation I had been brought up in. Always feeling alienated and never able to identify with the community around me. But why? Was there a community? Different from the older parts of Manchester and some of the towns of northern England, there was no sense of community and I never experienced the feeling of belonging in my particular part of Manchester. Negative thoughts are readily ascribed to any situation, but for me those negative thoughts were compounded by the positive aspiration to be Welsh. My experiences as a child in not understanding my mother's

61

conversations with her family; the sense of community and belonging in Llanberis; and the stimulating physical environment of the area, all combined to underline my identification with Wales and its culture.

No member of either side of the family had ever progressed to further education and when at the age of eighteen I was deemed fit to be university material, the guidance given me by the school was never doubted nor indeed questioned. My mother's influence led me to medicine. The school's guidance led me to the medical school in Manchester. There my existence as a weekend and holiday commuter progressed, the main difference now being that the holidays got longer and I could spend even more time in Wales. Living in a variety of flats in suburban south Manchester—leaving my father to his unnecessarily meagre existence in the north—was now the pattern of my life and it reflected very closely that of my contemporaries; a period at home alternating with a period of self-inquisition and learning at university.

But there the likeness ended. For me the self-inquisition led down a different path to most. Wales and Welshness meant little to any of my contemporaries. As the months slipped by, my disillusionment at the lack of sympathy and understanding of the situation in Wales from the next generation of potential leaders in England became total. This was the period, more than any other, which made me a nationalist; a pacific Welsh nationalist based on the very simple principle of pragmatic self-defence. If the next generation of Welsh people did not take on the responsibility of self-determination and propagation of Welsh culture, no one else would.

Reinforcing my own increasing commitment to Wales at this time was my attempt to learn Welsh. Although the sounds and simple phrases were there, only by attending night classes in 'spare time' at university, reinforced by practical experience at the weekend, one week in Coleg Harlech and occasional forays into *Teach Yourself Welsh* was I able to master the language adequately.

Whilst at university I met and married Dorothi, a student of speech therapy from Armagh in Ireland. The possibility of a repeat scenario of my childhood was clear. It is vital that sensitive areas, such as language, so important to the atmosphere of the home and the raising of children, are resolved at an early stage. My wish was to enable any children we might have in the future to be brought up fluent in Welsh and confident in their Welshness. Dorothi's outlook was totally compatible. Never having visited Wales prior to meeting me, her knowledge of Welsh was non-existent. Her success in many ways surpasses my own. From a totally unrelated background, not only did she learn Welsh but came to

62

be Head of Department for Speech Therapy in Gwynedd, a field where language is so vital in therapy and communication. Language is never a barrier if the attitude is right and the commitment is real.

Having qualified in medicine at the age of twenty-three, in common with all young doctors there follows a period of pre- and post-registration training. Having done my house-jobs in Manchester, I chose to work in the former chest-disease hospital at Llangwyfan in Clwyd. In Dyffryn Clwyd, for the first time ever, I made the first faltering steps in using Welsh in a professional setting. I recall the response from the staff: supportive but uncertain for few learned Welsh as a second language at that time. Without any doubt, however, the most important element in the equation, the patient, invariably appreciated it.

A year later I found myself back in Manchester doing a post-graduate degree in Radiation Therapy at the Christie Institute. Welsh was again of value when patients from the Wrexham catchment area, including Meirionydd, were frequently admitted to the wards. Dorothi and I were now living in a hospital flat and our first son, Dafydd Ieuan, was born on St. David's Day, 1969.

In many ways Dafydd's arrival focused our minds. Our existence was the very antithesis of what we wanted for our family; a community, roots and a Welsh environment. Early in 1970, the opportunity arose for us to change direction. On duty one Saturday morning, and sitting in the doctors' common-room, I picked up the weekly *British Medical Journal*. There appeared the advertisement which was to change my life and give us as a family the roots which we had sought. On offer was a single-handed dispensing practice in the village of Llanaelhaearn (population 250) in the Llŷn peninsula—total practice population 1,200.

The 1961 census showed the practice to be 93% Welsh-speaking. As I was later to find out, 100% of the indigenous population spoke Welsh. It was not an area I knew well but having persuaded the local Practitioner Committee that my commitment could more than make up for my relative inexperience, Dorothi and I moved to Llanaelhaearn in 1970.

Llanaelhaearn was to be our home—a very happy home—for the next ten years. Three more children were born there: Rhiannon Ceiri (1971), Angharad Elidir (1973) and Cian Ciarán (the Irish influence won through, 1976). The surgery and dispensary were in our home and Dorothi's Welsh, not to mention mine, improved by the day as patients called and rang.

Neither of us will ever forget the welcome to Llanaelhaearn, and for several weeks we were showered with welcoming gifts: tea, sugar, cakes, crafts and toys for Dafydd. Kindness from every direction. If we had

Apêl Tŷ'r *Faner*, Ymddiriedolaeth Nant Gwrtheyrn, by Robin Llwyd ab Owain.

needed any persuasion that we had made the right move it was there for all to see. The community made an indelible mark on us both. There was one exception. On the second night of my very first week in practice, a patient with a broad English accent walked in. He welcomed me as had everyone else but then, with my mouth wide open in amazement, he added: 'I'm sure you will enjoy it here. It's not a bad place apart from the bloody language'! Sitting in my doctor's surgery, how was I to respond? Trying to keep some sort of professional dignity, all I could mumble was, 'Oh, that's interesting—it's one of the main reasons I came here.'

Within two weeks of our arrival in Llanaelhaearn a public meeting was held in the village to discuss the future of the village school. It was threatened with closure—second on the list of 17 schools scheduled for closure following Caernarfon County Council's adoption of the Gittin's Report on primary education. All rural schools with fewer than 50 pupils and three teachers were to close.

One of the main pivots of village life was threatened. Within three months the local bus service to Nefyn ceased, and within six months my role as the quarry doctor came to an end as the last granite quarry in the area closed. In parallel, a village chapel was threatened. There had been seven shops in Llanaelhaearn at one time—now there was one.

It seemed that many of the features of the area that had attracted us were under threat. There was a very forceful campaign to keep the school open, although nobody believed it possible as we went to and fro to Caernarfon to lobby the education authority. Repeatedly the response I could hear locally was, 'Doctor, why do you trouble yourself; they will close it anyway?' But they didn't, and that single decision influenced much to come in Llanaelhaearn. An organisation, *Cymdeithas y Pentrefwyr* (Villagers' Association), was developed to try to create conditions more favourable for the village's future. The theory went that if we didn't solve the root cause of the village's problem—lack of work and depopulation—the threat to the school, and indeed other services, would raise its head again in the course of time.

Various problems were tackled, but despite good will from public authorities, little was fulfilled. There was an element of naïvity in our campaign. When all is said and done, why should any local authority look to support a small village of 250 people, more than any one of the other 200 and more villages of similar size in the old county of Caernarfon.

We had to do more to give direction and support ourselves. Another villager and myself visited the west coast of Ireland to look for ideas. On returning, a successful meeting was held in the old village memorial hall and *Antur Aelhaearn* was born. It was registered in January 1974 as the first community co-operative in the United Kingdom. I became the first chairman.

A branch of the *Urdd* was established and the first village eisteddfod for half a century was held. Land was obtained and we built our own factory, trained our own personnel and established two small home-craft industries. The factory was let to a company from Birmingham employing local labour in enamelling work. It lasted six months. So much for the commitment from branch factories. Their departure created a crisis for us with an empty factory on our hands. With some further thought, the home-craft industries were moved into the factory and developed there. Knitwear survived, pottery was less successful and after four years was no longer felt to be viable. The knitwear flourished in the factory for thirteen years, and at the peak eleven villagers were employed with many outworkers based at home.

In 1988 *Antur* took the decision to change direction and became a Local Development Trust. In 1989 *Antur* completed a joint venture with the Welsh Development Agency and Gwynedd County Council in establishing a training centre for young people in Dwyfor. The original factory accommodation is now twice the size, some 4,000 square feet. The development cost *Antur Aelhaearn* £130,000 and now provides much needed training facilities for the area, with up to three dozen people capable of being trained at any one time.

Antur Aelhaearn was established to try to create an alternative economic base for the area, and it acted as an important catalyst for debate in the mid 1970s. Prior to the Second World War, the granite quarries along the northern coast of Llŷn had employed up to 2,000 people. Agriculture had seen a parallel decline in employment. The vacuum as a result was considerable.

One of the casualties of the decline in quarrying in the area was the nearby coastal village of Porth-y-Nant in Nant Gwrtheyrn. The village had been built in the 1870s to house migrant workers developing the quarrying opportunities on the northern coast. Now it lay empty, the last occupants having moved out in 1959. Set in one of the most dramatic locations in Wales, the village of Porth-y-Nant was in the hands of a distant quarrying company. Few people visited the area at that time. Most who did referred to it as the 'ghost village'. For me it was an asset, which could be used to benefit the area.

In 1967 the Welsh Language Act was passed. This gave status to the language, albeit on a very limited basis, for the first time ever. Many local authorities and public bodies responded with tentative policies supportive of the language. In some areas most of these were difficult to implement, particularly in regard to appointing appropriately trained and bilingual staff. There was a need for some sort of a 'machine' to Cymricise those who wished to avail themselves of such a facility. Suddenly the whole came together.

If Nant Gwrtheyrn could be returned to our hands a language centre could be created, and employment and confidence in the area boosted at the same time. In 1972 I wrote to the owners of Nant—Amalgamated Roadstone—and asked if they were interested in selling. Six years later, after many public meetings, petitions and much lobbying, Nant Gwrtheyrn was sold to the Trust I had established in the mid 1970s. Over one-hundred other organisations and individuals had shown interest in buying the village, but ours, to the best of my knowledge, was the only one from Wales. Our success was a great boost for morale but, as the last ten years have shown, the hard work was only just beginning.

The village is now facing completion as the National Language Centre of Wales. Over 2,000 people were resident at the centre in 1989 alone. It has become a centre for the people, supported by the people. It has cost over £1 million to develop to date, much of that money being raised by the many thousands of people, both Welsh speakers and non-Welsh speakers, throughout Wales and beyond who have supported its aims.

One notable and lasting feature of the centre is the broad base of support we have received, crossing all political persuasions, religious and other divides. Nant Gwrtheyrn's standing has also been recognised by the acceptance by the European Bureau for Lesser-Used Languages, and in turn the European Community, of the role of Nant Gwrtheyrn as a specialist and co-ordinating centre for adult teaching of the lesser-used languages of Europe. At the time of writing, the Plas in Nant Gwrtheyrn is being developed to fulfil this role. European co-operation is vital as we enter the 1990s with the increased opportunities for cultural interchange and the potential to learn by each other's experiences.

Where does 'discovering Welshness' begin and end? It has been an evolutionary process for me. In 1983 several of us came together at the National Eisteddfod in Llangefni to discuss the role of Wales in the world—specifically by twinning with one of the Developing World's small African countries. In 1985 *Dolen Cymru* was established as a twinning between Wales and Lesotho, and in my capacity as chairman of the organisation I have tried to ensure that Wales' horizon is extended to include areas of development beyond our normal everyday preoccupations. Visits and exchanges between individuals, schools, churches and other organisations in both countries have ensured·greater understanding and friendship measured in wider parameters than traditionally seen. This is the first such twinning of any two countries anywhere in the world, and Wales' success in pioneering this relationship gives me particular pleasure. It has turned Wales' smallness and, dare I say it, insignificance in world terms on its head and used it to advantage. Our big brother the other side of Offa's Dyke could never have engaged in such a twinning, the politics of size and influence would never have allowed it. Small can be beautiful, and for me, as for many others, a new Welshness was discovered as a consequence.

It is often said that one of the great weaknesses of Wales is our capacity to argue amongst ourselves. With the establishment of the National Language Forum in May 1988, twelve of the front-line organisations in Wales came together to discuss the fate of the language. Traditionally they have often vied in public on various important issues. Various shades of opinion, from the National Eisteddfod, with its innate conservatism, to the radical lobbyists of *Cymdeithas yr Iaith* have been brought together in one cohesive forum. At a time when a new Welsh Language Act is being discussed, the need for a concerted voice and campaign to ensure the language's future is more vital than ever. As chairman of this National Forum, its greatest contribution is, in my opinion, still to come. It has matured over the years and the original membership has now risen to a figure of twenty-six. Too often in the past we have been divided and ruled. This new co-operation augers well for the future.

If anyone had said twenty years ago that I would have experienced the development of the above movements and been chairman of each in turn, there would have been more than a sideways glance. Life has, however, been very kind and the opportunities to 'discover Welshness' have been taken at each turn.

In contributing these few thoughts, one inevitably asks are there any conclusions to be drawn? Nobody is born speaking Welsh! All those who do speak it learn it at different stages in life, and to a different degree of fluency. In the same way, I would argue that 'discovering Welshness' is a phenomenon that can take place at different stages in an individual's life. It is dependent upon circumstances, family and environment.

Discovering Welshness is a phenomenon that can be attributed to fluent Welsh speakers, born and bred, and non-Welsh speakers alike. Many native Welsh speakers admit that they have not appreciated the significance of their inheritance until leaving home, or being challenged in some way. On the other hand, I know of very few non-Welsh speakers who, having 'discovered Welshness', do not then make an effort to learn the national language of Wales.

Despite all the prophecies of gloom and doom for the future of the language, I am constantly amazed at the capacity of Wales to evolve and adapt and to rediscover its Welshness. If discovering Welshness is an evolutionary phenomenon, so too is Welshness itself. As we approach the twenty-first century, I am convinced that our success as a people has to be one of the unsung success stories of cultural survival in Europe. Long may that success continue. 'Where there is no vision, the people shall perish.'

NANT GWRTHEYRN
R. S. Thomas

I listen to the echoes
of John Jones crying: 'God
is not good' and of his wife
correcting him: 'Hush, John.'

The cuckoo returns
to Gwrtheyrn, contradicting
John Jones, within its voice
bluebells tolling over

the blue sea. There is work
here still, quarrying
for an ancient language
to bring it to the light

from under the years'
dust covering it. Men,
with no palate for fine
words, they helped them down

with their sweat, spitting
them out later in what
served them for prayer. Was
it for this God numbered

their days? Where once pick-
axes would question, now
only the stream ticks, telling
a still time to listeners

at their text-books. Turning
its back on the world,
contemplating without boredom
unchanging horizons this place

knows a truth, for here
is the resurrection
of things. One after one
they arise in answer

to names they are called by,
standing around, shining,
by brief graves from whose hold
willing hands have released them.

'HERE IN ENGLAND'
Suzanne Greenslade

I am American and I have lived in several countries, including Japan, Spain and Italy. Now, with my Welsh husband, and daughter who carries dual nationality, I live in Wales, although I have kept my American citizenship. Learning Welsh in turn introduced me to Wales, which was very important for me. It has enriched my world perspective in the same way that my previous experience of learning other languages had done.

I cannot imagine why the actress Glenda Jackson, who is not Welsh-speaking, would say (HTV, 'Art & Soul', 13 April 1989) that she has 'doubts about Welsh being a language that is sufficiently expressive'. I have heard other people admit similar doubts about the Welsh language. Welsh, as far as I can see, is as expressive as any language I have spoken and is as vigorous as any language of which I am aware.

When I arrived in Wales in 1985 I approached the language in the same way as I would in any other nation with its own distinctive language and culture. I plunged myself into learning the customs of my new home. This was not the first time that I had found myself in a challenging social environment so I was well aware that the 'full immersion' technique would open many doors for me. So far, my instincts have been proven right.

I left my native Atlanta, Georgia, in November 1985, travelling in a van to New York City. From New York by ship to Southampton, then by van again to my husband's home in Cefn Cribwr, Mid Glamorgan.

71

We arrived on Thursday, 28 November, Thanksgiving Day and I felt very much like a Pilgrim in reverse. Two months later, in January 1986, I began Chris Rees's ingenious Wlpan-style Welsh course in Cardiff. I was six months pregnant at the time, but the fifty-mile round trip drive gave me a chance to review each daily lesson in the car.

At first Cefn Cribwr did not appear to be a particularly Welsh-speaking village. However, when my neighbours and new friends could see that I was absolutely serious about speaking Welsh, the local, rich Glamorgan dialect started coming at me from a variety of directions. My mother-in-law, who hadn't transferred the language to her sons, resurrected her Welsh after a silence of over thirty years. Her mother-in-law did the same, as did quite a few other old timers. I became a member of the chapel and began to understand more of the bilingual services and could sing the Welsh hymns with confidence. As a learner, I began attending specifically Welsh events such as eisteddfodau, *nosweithiau llawen*[1] and *cymanfaoedd canu*.[2] I had never experienced anything like a *cymanfa ganu* before and still, to me, it is one of the most powerful of all Welsh events.

The birth of my first child in March 1986 meant that I missed the end of the first-year Wlpan course, but I continued to study the language from other sources. By the time my daughter was a year old, Welsh and English were both used in our home. My husband, also a learner, continued to attend courses and to add to our use of the language. Our shelf of Welsh-language childrens' books grew, and our ability to subscribe to Welsh magazines, select tapes, records and television programmes improved. And by now the new friendships we had formed included a number of Welsh-speaking families who were also willing to help us along.

At this time I started full-time work as a photography lecturer in Swansea. Suddenly I was thrust out of the community atmosphere of Cefn Cribwr into an English-dominated working environment where 'things Welsh' were openly considered to be anachronistic and unworthy of serious attention. The overwhelming majority of my colleagues came from England. I, an American, was the only Welsh-speaking staff member in the department!

If a conversation related to the language were to come up, and I expressed a sympathetic view, I found myself being labelled a Welsh Nationalist and a supporter of *Meibion Glyndŵr* (whom I hadn't even heard of at that time). I soon learned to keep my mouth shut about the

[1] *noson lawen*: an evening of light and largely local entertainment
[2] song festivals

culture I had grown to love, and I had to bite my tongue whenever my colleagues said, 'Here in England'. In the face of such judgementalism, I find that I must struggle to keep my sense of humour and original enthusiasm. I feel that the linguistic situation in Wales is sometimes abnormal and absurd. Even now I find myself in a conversation struggling in broken Welsh with someone whom I know speaks English as well as I do.

My experiences as a seasoned traveller and as a language student in Madrid, Rome and Tokyo are of little help to me in understanding the situation here in Wales. Previously it was always I, as a newcomer, who had to adapt to local customs of diet, dress, etiquette and expression. In Japan I spoke Japanese and thus was able to communicate more deeply with my Japanese friends. In marked contrast, however, I recall meeting an Oxford Latin graduate who adamantly refused to learn Japanese. When I suggested that he should consider it, he accused me of 'collecting languages' as though learning the language were a vice.

It has consistently been my experience that those who take the trouble to learn the language of the country in which they live, whether Spanish in Spain or French in Cajun Louisiana, become part of that community. Bridges are built between the individual and the group as a result of a willingness to honour the local language.

In Wales I have been challenged to understand why Welsh speakers cling to the language preference that they have. It is also a challenge for me to understand why so many non-Welsh speakers have decided that Welsh could not possibly be 'sufficiently expressive'. This latter view is the most difficult to fathom as it leads to sanctions against the language that impose themselves on my Welsh-speaking family.

I now speak Welsh, yet in Ogwr, where I live, this ability is regarded with suspicion. In 1988 the Council passed a resolution that 'Council's business, including contact with the public will not be in Welsh or bilingual'. At the time of writing (December 1989) Ogwr Borough Council has still not overturned this official local government decision.

In spite of some very real obstacles and occasional disappointments, through learning Welsh I have gained some wonderful introductions into a rich and contemporary culture. It is sometimes difficult to strike a balance when living in two separate worlds—obstinately English-only at work, yet using our choice of languages at home. Through the language of our daughter's Welsh nursery school new doors are opening all the time. I feel that with her help my immersion into Wales will be a natural and harmonious one. It would be wrong, I feel, if future generations were made to feel that the language they speak were somehow substandard or inferior to any other language in the world.

WELSH HILLS
Oliver Davies

The moment of my conversion to Welshness came, I remember, when I was standing in the hot sun in open fields some seven-hundred miles south of Moscow. Quite why this should have been so, I have never understood. And what triggered the response? Certainly not the view; there is a sense of space in the plains of southern Russia which we do not have in Wales. But there was a lifting of the heart, which would certainly have been congenial to my Russian friends (had I shared my experience with them at the time), however obscure its rationale.

And the way in which that conversion was mediated to me was through a vision: quite simply, I saw hills. Not Alps, nor the steep wooded hills of the Caucasus, but low, green hills of the type that I walked with my father as a small boy on Sunday afternoons, vaguely feeling that this was a good thing to do, and enjoying it all, vaguely. Then my world would become a world of turf, of wind, of sky, as I plodded with my father up some *bryn* or other, wholly unaware that I was absorbing sensations which were to become memories that would thrust their way into my adolescent mind at a place and time far removed.

Wales remains for me a place of hills. There is, for instance, that great, long hill of the Welsh language up which I labour, in the company of thousands, envious of those virtuosic mountaineers who trip lightly from pinnacle to pinnacle in the remote distance. And then there are those other, miraculous hills which are the first sight to greet me and my wife every morning when we wake. Carnedd Dafydd, tipped with cloud; the Glyderau, green and sheer; the jagged outline of Braich Tŷ Du, new-born, spilling cloud into the Nant Ffrancon valley below. It is a view which sets everything into proportion, which enlivens and redeems.

Wales, the land of hills. And the Welsh, it seems to me, are—like all inhabitants of mountainous lands—fundamentally a valley people. We have a gift for community, for weaving intricate tapestries of relations and relatedness, for giving each other names. Each and every one belongs to a family, a street, a *bro* (and if such are lacking, then they will be provided). That is what we might call the *horizontal* plane of community. Of course, there are other cultures where a similar sense of community exists: societies which, like the Welsh, have experienced centuries of hard industrial and rural life which creates a powerful feeling of interdependence: the subterranean sense that life is best faced together. There are other organic communities. But there exists another dimension in Wales, which is quite special and very precious and whose like cannot so easily be found among other peoples. This is what we might call the *vertical* plane of our community, and it is the gift of our culture and the language which supports it.

Precisely because our corporate identity is inextricably bound up with a language, achievements in and through language are a fundamental part of our national consciousness; and it is the poets who are the true heroes. It is the poetic tradition which, far more than a catalogue of dates, articulates the historical consciousness of the people; and it is the poets who, rooted through their craft in a tradition which is both ancient and virile, become the foci of historical community. If the historical continuity of England is expressed most clearly through institutions, then the historical continuity of the Welsh is most present in the poets' living word.

Born of a Welsh-speaking father and an English mother, I grew up in anglicised south Wales; and hence can regard myself as a child of that union of cultures which is so widespread today and which can constitute such a threat to Welsh Wales. My teens were spent in Cardiff where (rightly or wrongly) it seemed that I was living in a kind of Welsh-flavoured England. Wales (though very, very close) was in a sense a foreign country. Many of us had Welsh surnames, all of us were fanatical supporters of rugby players in red, but we knew in our heart of hearts that we were 'not really Welsh' (and all attempts to teach the language to us, or indeed, the history of Wales only seemed to confirm this). And we felt this way, of course, because there were a handful of children in our midst who spoke Welsh and whose experience of Welshness was palpably different from our own. How could we ever claim to be one of 'them' when what made them 'really Welsh' was precisely that language which we did not know? Welsh—those familiar but incomprehensible words—seemed an unbridgeable barrier between what they were and what we were: their fate and ours.

And yet, marvellously, languages can be learned. Which is what I did. At the age of fifteen or so. I picked up Caradar's *Welsh Made Easy* and began to speak halting Welsh to my father, who imparted to me his (by now slightly threadbare) Carmarthenshire dialect. And those early months remain in my mind as a time of glory; quite suddenly I seemed to be becoming 'really Welsh' in that more precious way. I shall never forget the sheer thrill of answering the question 'Do you speak Welsh?' in the affirmative for the very first time: 'Yes, I do'— *Ydw, rwy'n siarad Cymraeg*.

I have learned many things since then, of course. Welshness is not just a language; it is the whole *civilisation* which that language supports, and which takes a lifetime to get to know. I have discovered that Welshness roots me in the past in a way that was not an option for me, personally, through Englishness. It has given me a history of poets rather than kings and queens. It has allowed me to identify with those who have suffered the 'flip-side' of history (in Gutierrez's phrase). Welshness has given me a present too, one in which I feel, as a Welsh speaker, that I have a contribution to make, in which there are battles to be fought which must be won. It has given me a warm companionship with others in shared commitment to a truly just cause. But most of all, Welshness has given me a particular sense of the future. Old imperialisms—East and West— are being broken down. The inherited models no longer work as they did; and change is in the air. The British Empire has withdrawn and exists now only in the minds and hearts of too many Britons, where it must be supplanted by a new vision of cultural dialogue and pluralism. I hope and believe that we are entering a new age in which what is local and communitarian, what is small and *human*, will receive the respect it is due. In each context in a different way, this is a battle which is being fought all over the world; but it is being fought with a particular urgency —around the cause of Welshness—in this place of Wales, and in a way that concerns us all.

TALLEY ABBEY
Oliver Davies

I chanced upon your grave
Above the water
In green Talyllychau
Dafydd: *bardd mwyaf Cymru.*

A man who lit the candle of his world
With soft-bellied words of sap and fire
Who carved curved surfaces of air
In light-drift song, who uttered
In intricate melodies of meaning,
Concrete patterns of irridescent colour,
Caverns of sound and concave echoes
That preached redemption
By breath of vowels,
Cut and coupled edge
Of wild-won, winsome consonants,
Free worked and full wracked.

Dafydd of the weaving breath,
Who skilled the inner mastery
Of song and celebration, whose
Green cunning spindled
Life webs of willowed words.

I chanced upon your grave
Above the water
In green Talyllychau
Where silence gathers to a knot
Tight, in the soil's depth,
Like breath that is denied,
Where the sun splintered by trees,
Streaks with living yellow
The taut and stream-lined surface
Of remembered realities.

Beneath the yew tree, Dafydd,
Above the water
In the green bed of Talyllychau
You sleep, Dafydd,
And dream of us:
Your strange progeny.

Dafydd ap Gwilym, Talyllychau, by Fiona Bowie

HOBSON'S CHOICE
Zonia Bowen

I was born in Norfolk of English parents, brought up in Yorkshire, and first came to Wales in 1943 at the age of seventeen as a student at the University College of North Wales, Bangor. When I filled in my application form to go there, the fact that Bangor was in Wales didn't really mean anything to me, and I didn't even know that there was such a language as Welsh. I had chosen Bangor because I hated large towns such as Leeds, the nearest university town to my home, and had decided that if I were going to spend four years somewhere, I may as well choose a place near sea and mountains and away from factories and smoky chimneys.

University Hall, now Neuadd John Morris-Jones and the hall of residence for Welsh-speaking students was, at that time, a hostel for women students in general. There I found myself sharing a room, divided into four cubicles, with Jean from Liverpool and two Welsh girls, both called Elizabeth, or Betty and Beti-Wyn for short. I suppose it would have been natural to think that the two Welsh girls would pal up together, and that the two from the North of England would do likewise, but it didn't work out quite like that and, although we all got on very well together, Betty from Mynytho became my special friend and remained so throughout our four years in college.

At that time there were only 300 or so students in the whole college, about half of them Welsh-speaking. Most of the Welsh speakers had opted for the Arts subjects, as I had.

Jean was the only one of my room-mates who was studying Science, so we didn't see much of her during the day. The two Elizabeths, who spoke Welsh to each other, were both taking Welsh as their main subject and I was taking French, but all three of us attended the same lectures in English, History and Latin, and the compulsory Physical Education which all intending teachers had to take even during their first year, so it was only natural that I found myself going back and forth with the Welsh girls and their other friends, and attending the same social events of an evening.

We also sat together for meals in the hostel dining room, and it was here that I first realised that I was at a disadvantage, with all the others laughing and talking together in Welsh, and my not being able to understand what was going on.

I remember how during one of the first days I was sitting in my cubicle reading, when I heard Beti-Wyn from Porthmadog quietly singing to herself in her own cubicle. I didn't understand the words of '*Bugeilio'r Gwenith Gwyn*', but the song had a wistful melody. I conjured up the picture of a young mother sitting in a lonely cottage in the Outer Hebrides crooning softly to her baby, and I was enchanted. I asked Beti-Wyn to write the words down and explain them to me.

At the Saturday morning sing-songs organised by the students I heard other songs of a different nature, some of them popular ones in Welsh tradition such as '*Sosban Fach*', or parodies on well-known hymns with quite different, less respectful lyrics substituted for the original ones. There were songs in English as well as in Welsh, but once again I realised that my friends were enjoying themselves twice as much as I was, because I could only understand half of what was going on.

Some events were entirely in Welsh of course, such as the *nosweithiau llawen,*—'merry evenings', with songs, jokes, sketches and general acting the fool by groups of students to entertain the others, or the more serious Welsh plays put on from time to time by the Welsh drama group. I had the choice of going along and trying to understand what I could, or staying away altogether whilst my friends went out to enjoy themselves. I usually decided to go along and even joined the women's and mixed Welsh choirs when they competed in the Inter-College Eisteddfod.

There were things outside college too, the *Urdd* (Welsh League of Youth) eisteddfod, various social events at the Welsh chapels which my friends attended, and being asked out to tea with my friends by various Welsh relatives and acquaintances. I found that being bilingual they could all enter into my world, but that I couldn't enter into theirs. What an advantage and pleasure it must be to be able to understand and speak both languages!

Of course, I understood certain words adapted from English which seemed to spatter every conversation and, after hearing a Welsh broadcast one day, I remember asking them the silly question: 'Are all Welsh verbs the same as English verbs with "-io" added?'

However, I mustn't give the impression that Welsh was the main medium of our college life. English was the language of all our lectures, official communications, and most social events and college society meetings. We went to see English plays and took part in English debates. I cannot understand people who think that taking an interest in the Welsh language and Welsh affairs somehow means that one is narrow-minded and parochial. Surely, knowing more than one language widens rather than narrows one's experience? We hear much talk about Welsh creating a language barrier, but it is not the knowledge of Welsh that creates the barrier, but the lack of knowledge of it.

The first time I ever remember seeing Welsh in print was when I picked up a copy of the newspaper *Y Cymro* in the students' common room, and wondered how one pronounced words without any vowels in them, such as *'cwm'* and *'bwthyn'*, until I learned that 'w' and 'y' were indeed vowels in Welsh, representing sounds similar to 'u' and 'i' in English, and that the Welsh letter 'u' represented quite a different sound somewhere half way between the two.

Maybe one reason I wanted to identify myself with the Welsh students was that during the war the college buildings, as indeed lectures and lecturers, were shared with another university,—the University of London, and there was much friendly rivalry between the two sets of students, at football matches, boat races on the Menai and other similar contests between the two colleges. Being a member of the University of Wales, I, of course, always shouted for the Welsh team and joined in the college yell,—which was naturally in Welsh. I must admit, too, that I took some pleasure in the one-upmanship of our Welsh teams being able to shout advice to each other in Welsh, which the monoglot teams couldn't understand.

At the time there were no Welsh classes in college or even in town for any one like me wanting to learn Welsh, nor, I regret to say, did I get much direct help from my Welsh friends, even though most of them were studying to become Welsh teachers. No one offered to take me in hand and give me Welsh lessons, even once a week. So there was nothing for it but to buy books and study the language on my own. But I suppose my friends did help in some way by speaking to each other in their own language and occasionally answering my questions about pronounciation and meaning. There were no cassettes in those days!

The first book I bought was *Welsh in a Week*. It took me far more than a week to master the language, of course, but even learning phrases like 'Good morning', 'How are you?', 'Please' and 'Thank you' is a start. The second and only other book I ever bought to learn Welsh was *Welsh Made Easy* by Caradar. Looking back at it today it looks rather dry and uninteresting, with no illustrations and small print, but I still think it is one of the best instruction manuals ever written on the subject. I remember sitting in my grandfather's garden during the long summer holidays, which always seemed to be hot and sunny in those days, going through the book and reciting Welsh phrases over and over to myself. No, you can't learn any language without hard work and dedication. That is where incentive is important. If you are keen enough you will enjoy the effort and hard work, and the more languages one learns the easier it becomes to learn a new one. Therefore, as I have found, learning Welsh is a help to learning other languages, not an impediment.

During my fourth year in college I was sent to do teaching practice in various schools in Bangor and Caernarfon, and I realised with delight just how fluent children of seven and eight could be in two languages, and how important it was that their teachers should also be fluent in both, which I wasn't at that time, of course.

One day one of our Education lecturers came into the classroom to listen to me teaching. After giving my lesson I set the children some work and walked round the class giving help to different children here and there where needed. I passed close to where the lecturer was sitting at the back of the class scribbling away in his notebook as he had been doing throughout the lesson, and I tried to take a sideways glance at what he was writing, fearing that he was making some adverse comments about my teaching. To my amusement I found that he wasn't making notes about my lesson at all, but doing the written exercises in Caradar's *Welsh Made Easy*!

It was during my last year at college that I met Geraint who had returned after the war to complete his training as a teacher. Here, at last, was somebody who actually spoke to *me* in Welsh and had patience to listen as I struggled to reply to him in his own language, and better still to correct my mistakes!

My friends seemed to regard with great respect the fact that Geraint had won the Chair at the National Eisteddfod. This meant nothing at all to me at the time, because I didn't really know what a National Eisteddfod was, or what winning the Chair meant, but I later went with Geraint to the National Eisteddfod at Colwyn Bay, and was introduced to all the facets of Welsh cultural life, poetry competitions, *Gorsedd* ceremonies, male-voice choirs, harp playing, *penillion* singing . . .

I had heard *penillion* singing in college, of course, and must admit that for a while I found it rather annoying to hear the harp start to play a beautiful melody only to hear the voice suddenly coming in to drown it with quite a different melody, which didn't seem even tuneful. But as I began to understand more and more of the words which were sung I also began to appreciate the artistry involved in using the background melody to give appropriate expression to the words. Now it is one of my favourite types of singing, which all goes to illustrate that we shouldn't be too quick to judge things which we really know nothing about.

If we are living in Wales we are missing a very great deal if we close our eyes to the traditional culture and language. Nor does learning about them mean that we cannot also enjoy the treasures of English culture. We can have the best of both worlds. I wanted my children too to enjoy these advantages.

When our first child was born we were living in the large village of Rhosllannerchrugog near Wrexham in a Welsh-speaking community. We found ourselves sharing a rented house with another young couple whom we hadn't known previously, but who were also Welsh-speaking. Their first baby arrived a week after ours. All their relatives who called to see them spoke Welsh and so did Geraint's colleagues at the local grammar school and their wives who visited us. All our new friends spoke the same language, and it seemed the most natural thing in the world that we should speak Welsh to our own son. As his vocabulary grew, so did mine.

The next ten years or so of our life was spent in more anglicised areas near Wrexham and Cardiff, but we were fortunate in being able to send our children to Welsh-medium schools where it was the policy to make sure that the children entering school around the age of four or five were fluent in both languages by the age of eleven. We felt that a Welsh-medium education was necessary because there were so many counter-balancing influences,—playmates in neighbouring houses who were not Welsh-speaking, radio and, later, television. There was no S4C in those days.

I also got involved with Welsh nursery-school groups and parent-teacher associations. This involvement was a great help for me to practise speaking Welsh myself.

A few years after we were married Geraint was asked to take a Welsh evening class at the Wrexham Technical College. I didn't actually attend his class because one of us had to stay in to look after the children, but he put my name down to sit the O Level exam with the other students at the end of the course. I think this made me look more closely at my grammar and spelling and gave me more confidence, so that later on I ventured writing articles in Welsh for various magazines. In fact, I even started a Welsh women's magazine, *Y Wawr*, which I edited for over eight years. That was, of course, after I had started the women's movement *Merched y Wawr* in 1967 shortly after going to live in the tiny village of Parc, near Bala, Geraint having been moved to Meirionnydd as Inspector of Schools for that area.

I don't think it was till we moved there that I discovered what real Welshness was. For the first time I found myself living in a community which was almost a hundred percent Welsh-speaking, and where it was possible to live one's life from day to day without hearing or speaking any other language. I must admit that having come straight from south Wales where a slightly different brand of Welsh is spoken as far as intonation and odd words here and there are concerned, I had some difficulty at first in understanding, especially as some of the farmers in particular seemed to speak very quickly, but, thank goodness, no one ever dreamed of turning to English, and in a matter of weeks I was chattering back almost as fluently as they did.

Everybody knew everybody else. In fact, most of the inhabitants were related to each other in some way or another. Everyone was auntie or uncle to all the children and I, too, soon became auntie. We all called in on each other when passing each other's houses without needing any excuse or pretext, and we all went to help with the shearing or hay-making. Not that there is anything particularly Welsh about any of these activities in themselves, but Welsh was the natural and only language of communication. There were different social events taking place nearly every night, too, at which most of the entertainment was home produced, in Welsh naturally, as no one thought of speaking any other language.

There were many other such villages in Wales at the time, but things are changing rapidly now as more and more English people, like myself, move in to live in these villages,—and not all of us are willing to make the effort to learn Welsh. Do we really think that because all the native Welsh speakers have made the effort to learn our language that we have no need to reciprocate? Do we really realise that even one or two non-Welsh speakers in a village association such as a women's group, a youth club, a W.E.A. class, a village hall committee or a parent-teacher association can change the language of that association overnight and eventually the language of the whole community? Or are we willing to integrate, just as we would expect any Welsh person going to live in England to integrate into an English-language community? As far as I was concerned the choice was clear and I can't imagine how it could have been otherwise.

IN ENGLAND ISN'T IT?
Leigh Verrill-Rhys

My journey to Wales began in Ireland with bold Fenians, rising moons, red bees humming and Innisfree. Like many Americans, I was enamoured by the patriotic struggle for freedom, the stand against a stronger enemy, the hopeless and ever hopeful effort to regain a destroyed heritage. My ears were filled by the old lamenting folk songs, my heart ached for sad old Ireland, her mistreated people and her lilting grief. I listened hard to long-standing tales of injustice.

I believed that Irishness was Harrington's Irish Pub on the 17th of March after the big parade through downtown streets, wearing the green, drinking Guinness or Power's, Irish priests, and despising the oppressor. My reading of Yeats, Behan, Joyce and the rest did not contradict those early impressions. I had never set foot in Ireland, not in Bloom's Fair City nor distant Galway.

Instead, I arrived in Wales—for a few days one hot August. I cannot remember why I came. Ireland had begun to frighten me. The Troubles had started; I did not want to be that close to struggle. Wales was Celtic, at least, close to Ireland in that sense. Or was it that someone mentioned a museum they'd visited? The scenery? A green valley? The notice at the tourist office in Chester announcing a medieval market-day in Rhuthun?

Camelot, Arthur and castles—they were romantic—so I came. Somewhere on the bus route I waited at a tiny station for the connecting bus. Around me were women with shopping bags and children in tow. Nothing very romantic about them or the market day. I stood close to the curb, trying to appear uninterested in their conversations but listening closely to every sound. How could I have known that anywhere in Wales (isn't that in England?) the people would speak a language of their own? Scots Gaelic, yes. Irish, yes. Even Manx, but not Welsh.

In the United States, the Irish, the Scots and Manx count for a great deal of our heritage, but the Welsh, despite their numbers and contributions, keep a very low profile. St. David's Day is not on the calendar but St. Patrick's is. Very few Americans know where Wales is and fewer still, once myself included, have any idea what Welsh ('Welch' to us) is.

But Welsh it was in the bus station, on the street, in the market. I was all ears, excited and amazed. I had *seen* Irish, Scots Gaelic and Manx written, but here was a language I never imagined existed being used. I don't remember what superlative I used to describe this language but, being an American, it might well have been 'cute'!

At the first opportunity, in a museum someone mentioned, I bought a book and a dictionary. I was going to learn this language, teach myself.

The gnats in the park along the river to the west of the castle in Cardiff were horrible. I couldn't find any place to eat on Sunday evening. I felt guilty about having a bath because of the drought but I walked, tranquil and at home, along Cathedral Road once I understood which way to turn from the guest-house door. To here I knew I would return, somehow I was close to home.

Four years passed and without warning, I began to daydream about Wales. The spell that the language had cast resurfaced; my discovery of Welsh mythology and the origins of the Arthurian tales, which had so permeated Western romanticism, led me into embarrassing debates with professors.

I found my tourist's map, scouring it avidly for place-names and rivers, towns I had seen, legendary castles, mythic valleys. All forces in my life were at work; I had started a novel, some of the characters spoke Welsh and I began again to teach myself.

I got nowhere.

August came again and with it a Welsh Language Course in San Rafael. The novel was finished but I still had to work on the Welsh-language aspect. I did not want very much Welsh, just enough to make the novel convincing.

But once started, I could not stop.

The struggle for freedom, the stand against a stronger enemy, the ever hopeful effort to defend a living but besieged heritage. I bounded into the fray. I studied Welsh for another year; abandoned any plans to publish that novel—it would never be convincing; took a place on a two-year course in Pontypridd. I stayed in Wales, walking some part of Cathedral Road every day for months, but no longer tranquil nor at home.

During the year I studied Welsh in the States. I had joined the local Welsh-American Society, been introduced to Welsh Cakes and St. David's Day, *cymanfaoedd canu*[1] and *capel*.[2] Was Welshness then like Irishness? At meetings we sang hymns and folk tunes, learned a dance or two, wore red, white and green, compared family trees and discussed how close Roddy McDowell and Maureen O'Hara came to being the very image of a brother, a sister—or not at all!

[1] Singing festivals.
[2] Chapel.

In Cardiff, none of these *pethau Cymreig*[1] were of any importance. Here, the talk was of a fourth channel, starvation, joblessness, language rights. *Pethau* to sink your political teeth into, *pethau* few Welsh-society members wanted to know a word about.

Once started, I found myself constantly on the defensive. 'Why learn Welsh? Who ever heard of it?' 'Isn't that one of those wierd little Celtic languages? I thought it was dead.' 'It should be dead—dead and buried.' 'What do you ever hope to get out of *that?*'

But once here, I was completely lost. My native language failed me. My ability in Welsh was wholly inadequate. I understood no one who spoke to me. I could not make myself understood. Small things, ordinary everyday articles of necessity, catchphrases, and slang—none were the same. Language had always been my instrument and I was bereft. I did not care to change my English, my first language as it is spoken in my native country suited me fine. To find a place in my new home, I had to improve my Welsh.

I had a distinct advantage over most newcomers, I understood enough Welsh not to be frightened by posters and television programmes, or paranoid about conversations on buses. On my second visit I was full of questions about what names meant and how this or that was pronounced. I would not want to be a non-Welsh-speaking immigrant to Wales—that seems to me a barren land and lonely. Nor can I imagine the kind of soul who could chose to live in Wales without first learning something of her language. But then I came to Wales for the language, without Welsh there is no Wales for me at all.

I look back on my infatuation with Ireland now with embarrassment. I was too romantic to understand that its only weapon and best defence against the destruction of its heritage, rarely mentioned in the folk-singers' repertoire, is Gaelic. The language is given lip-service in government but its archaic script signals its complete inadequacy in the modern world. All the world drinks Guinness and sings to Molly Malone—what *was* Irish now drowned in bleary romanticism and sentimentality and futile violence.

Wales is its language. Welshness is entirely dependent on the existence of the language, otherwise it is a culture in translation—a shadow. Welsh cakes, laverbread and leeks, spontaneous miners' choruses singing '*Sosban Fach*' through the hills, Camelot—these are all filigree, insubstantial and fleeting against the onslaught of economic migration, technology and satellite television.

[1] Welsh matters.

Welshness is a child, a woman, a man speaking the language of their country—Welsh. Once it is gone there will be no joke in asking, 'Isn't that in England?'

RETURN OF THE NATIVE
Jeffrey Gainer

The village of Blaenllechau rests on the sunny side of the Rhondda Fach and there on the second day of October, 1951, was born a second son to Thomas William and Mary Gwenllian Gainer. That son am I. Blaenllechau itself has a short history. It was a mining village and was established in the middle of the last century when colliers tramped over the hill from the Cynon valley. Our family had lived in 'Blaen' (as the locals termed it) since the 1880s at least, and even today it remains a closely-knit community. The village formerly belonged to the ancient parish of Llantrisant and the nearest church was that of Llanwynno which has been made famous by Glanffrwd's work of the same name. In Llanwynno churchyard are buried my father's maternal grandparents and it might seem that any sense of being Welsh might also be said to have been appropriately interred there for at the tender age of four years the family removed to the industrial Midlands.

Coventry in the 1950s was a city that felt itself stirring into new life after the destruction brought about by the Second World War. True, ugly little pockets of war-damaged sites were to be found here and there in the city centre but prosperity brought by the expanding car industry meant that civic pride was shown in precinct and new cathedral. To this city came a motley crew: Geordies, Scots, Irish and Welsh and, thereafter, residents of the Caribbean and the Indian sub-continent. My upbringing was in many ways very English. Certainly English was the language of the home. My parents spoke nothing else or rather they had not been given the opportunity to speak anything else despite the fact that three of my four grandparents were fluent in Welsh. It appeared that a combination of concern for family tranquility—one grandfather was a native of Cheltenham—and the feeling that *yr iaith fain* (English) was more appropriate in days when Welsh was diminishing in use in the Valley communities, resulted in my parents being unable to speak the language. However, they could sing it! Indeed, one of my earliest memories is of my mother singing the occasional Welsh ditty. In latter years my father felt acutely the loss of the language and made attempts to master the complexities of mutation and syntax but his efforts were cut short by his death.

The outward course of my upbringing may therefore strike many as, for the most part, very English. After the home, the school plays an important role in mental and social formation. Bablake School, Coventry, which I attended between 1963 and 1969, is an ancient foundation. Isabella—not perhaps the most virtuous of English queens —had founded a Chantry College back in the fourteenth century. This ecclesiastical institution had changed in the course of time into a grammar school. I owe a great debt to Bablake School. Its academic standards were high and its dedicated staff implanted a love of English literature in me and encouraged a rather bookish teenager to work hard. There was a Welsh element of sorts—we seemed to have a succession of former Welsh rugby internationals on the staff! However, the education was, on the whole, very English in ethos. The only reference to Welsh culture I can recall was a hint in an A-level English class that a particular poem by Wilfred Owen might have been influenced by Welsh poetry.

And yet . . . and yet . . . whilst the school may have been very English, family roots cannot be so easily forgotten. A feeling for the place of birth remained and remains. Looking back, our family seemed to form part of a distinctive sub-community within the confines of Coventry. At the weekend we would welcome various relatives and friends who had also migrated from south Wales and gossip would concern, yes, the events of the day, but also the news from 'back home'. No doubt the feeling of being in exile has vanished for the generation after myself who have been assimilated, but even if we had not retained our ancestral language we were conscious of being Welsh just as our neighbours over the road who had moved from Dublin were likewise English speakers but in no sense English! Moreover the Welsh community in Coventry had a few centres, most notably the Welsh chapel in the city centre. Again our family liked to hear a visiting choir from the homeland whenever a Welsh concert was given at the Methodist Central Hall.

But if there was one thing that maintained the sense of Welshness it was the regular return visits 'back home'. The recollection of the earliest of such visits is lost in my subconscious. However, the return to 'Blaen' or Ferndale was always eagerly anticipated despite the lengthy journey —no two-hour dash down the motorway in the 1950s, to be sure! The sense of belonging to a particular place is most important: *brogarwch* (love of one's own patch) contributes greatly to *gwladgarwch* (love of one's homeland). This was exemplified in my mother's father. He was known locally as Dai Coch because of his shock of red hair. He had been born at Groeslon, near Caernarfon, at the turn of the century and after serving in the Belgium fields of blood in the First World War had been constrained to come south to find work in the pits of the South Wales Coalfield. However, he sought to return to Groeslon to visit his widowed mother and it was a source of great interest to me to visit his home—Crugan Ganol—in Groeslon some years ago. Much, therefore, can be done to stimulate a sense of Welshness by fostering a sense of association with place.

And the next place on my return to my Welsh roots was again, paradoxically, a quintessentially English city: Oxford. My school masters encouraged me in my studies and, being aware of my Welsh background, encouraged me to apply to Jesus College, Oxford, to read for a degree in Modern History. I was an undergraduate from 1970 to 1973. The college in those days—as no doubt today—was a fair mixture of plutocratic Southerners, sturdy North Country grammar-schoolboys and those from the Principality. The Principal, Hrothgar John Habbakuk, hailed from Barry and was a distinguished economic historian. Amongst the luminaries of the college was the Professor of Celtic, Idris Foster. Being almost entirely ignorant of Welsh literature (alas!) I was forced to rely upon a contemporary from Cardigan who would supply me with details of Sir Idris' interest in various aspects of Welsh culture. On one occasion—it may have been St. David's Day (always an occasion of great festivity in Jesus College)—the said contemporary berated me when I mispronounced virtually every word of '*Hen Wlad Fy Nhadau*', the Welsh National Anthem. This hurt my pride—not a bad thing—and made me realise that there was more to being Welsh than being nostalgic. Another Oxford contemporary was more concerned to establish a republic rather than maintain a Principality and departed from Oxford and found Celtic sustenance in Aberystwyth. This may have stimulated an awareness that national identity has to be maintained by more than ceremonial gestures. The years at Jesus College were, on the whole, exhilarating and, as before, the sense of being Welsh, though subdued, was still present. I was never a member of the Dafydd ap Gwilym Society—it was rumoured to be a rather curious gathering—as I was not eligible. The only languages apart from English that I studied at Oxford were Latin and German, and those simply to meet the requirement of the public examiners. However, the experiences of meeting Welsh speakers at University, of going along to

Welsh evensong each Thursday in the college chapel, of hearing about Welsh literature, all these things kindled in me a sense of loss.

There are, I think, many in Wales who feel this. In this century the Welsh language has lost ground and the recent forecasts that fairly early in the next century there will be few, if any, communities in Wales where the language will be spoken as the *primary* speech has filled some of us, at least, with sadness. There is, I believe, a deep connection between language and culture. A language moulds thought, expresses feeling, and connects the speaker thereof with all those who have spoken it down the ages. However, there is a world of difference between accepting these ideas as true and taking definite action to learn Welsh. What triggered off my resolve was a visit to Brittany shortly after ordination. At this time (1978) I was happily settling into a curacy at Baglan, Port Talbot. The return to Wales had appeared purely fortuitous. Who knows? Anyhow, the Principal of my theological college knew that if I moved over to Wales—I was then an ordinand sponsored by the Oxford diocese—he would be able to offer a place to a would-be student from the London diocese who had already had to wait a year because of lack of space at Wycliffe Hall. So it was in order to accommodate the organisation of a crowded theological college that the Principal contacted the Bishop of Llandaff, and in 1977 I found myself receiving ordination to the Apostolic Ministry not in Christchurch, Oxford, but in the venerable Christian site of Llandaff Cathedral, Cardiff. Some six months into the curacy, the church organist, Roger Chilcott, asked me if I would be interested in joining the Cymric Glee Choir (Aberafan) on a visit to Lorient, Brittany, where we would take part in an inter-Celtic festival. It was this visit that made me resolve to learn Welsh. I felt an awkwardness about representing Wales and not being able to speak a sentence of my national language. To be truthful, I also felt envious of those who could speak their own Celtic language. On returning home, therefore, I hastily purchased a few grammar books and elementary readers. It was to be a frustrating experience. The initial pleasure from analysing how a language works was mixed with a feeling of incompetence as I mangled the sounds. Fortunately, the Vicar of Baglan at the time, the Reverend David Islwyn Lewis, was a wonderful help. He was patient, tolerant and encouraging and after a few weeks we started to recite morning prayer together although I have never dared to ask him what he felt about my vain efforts at that time to pronounce such words as *archangylion* or *dyrchafodd*. Again certain parishoners were Welsh-speaking and gave me great encouragement, being willing to correct elementary errors of mine—such as *tri dynion* instead of *tri dyn*.

The pleasures that speaking Welsh has given me may be summed up in one word: discovery. It is as if a treasure were to be concealed just below the soil surface and then be unearthed. There is no substitute for obtaining the treasure—simply admiring photographs of it is not enough. So it is with the business of acquiring the Welsh language. It has disclosed so many interesting possibilities. May I indicate some?

(a) Social intercourse and parochial work

Recently it fell to my lot to visit Pontardawe on a parochial mission. It was a great asset to be able to speak Welsh, as the initial barrier of suspicion was broken down when the conversation turned to Welsh. People do value greatly the opportunity of speaking in their own tongue, and once that language is held in contempt it is tantamount to holding the speakers of the language in contempt too. It is crucial that the Church in Wales, which claims to be the historic Church of the land, should promote the use of Welsh and encourage its clergy to learn it.

Moreover the Welsh-speaking communities are invaluable. Language is not a private affair. Yes, George Steiner and others may point out that we all have our own idiolect—our own turn of phrase, vocabulary and so on—but nevertheless an idiolect only makes sense when it forms part of a widely perceived structure of communication called language. So it is vital that predominantly Welsh-speaking areas be maintained; whilst it is true that many in south Wales feel that they are Welsh whilst not speaking the language, their sense of cultural distinctiveness is due to the distinctiveness of the Welsh language and culture, which is, as it were, in the background. Once the background goes, sooner rather than later, the dependent sense of being Welsh will vanish too. A tradition—the transmission of a living language and all that goes with it—will have become merely a memory. We remember the dead but we are to be concerned with the living. This point is clearly seen in Ireland where the last few places where *Erse* is spoken (the so-called *Gaeltacht*) is threatened with extinction. Once that has happened Ireland will have lost something which only Ireland can give to the rest of the world—the reality of a living tradition. We must contend to promote the use of the Welsh language at all levels of society.

(b) A sense of community across time

Basic to the Christianity I profess is the conviction that we are all one in Christ. That means that the communion of saints is no mere phrase. Bishop Timothy Rees of Llandaff encapsulates what I mean when he says that the prayers of Dewi, Dyfrig, Teilo, Deiniol should sanctify the acres of our land. This continuum down the ages is part of the corporate awareness of the nation as well as of the Church. That is why it is so encouraging to note the burgeoning of interest in Welsh historical studies since the war. To be Welsh is to be aware of one's forefathers in this land. As I write these words my mind goes back to last Friday, the Feast of Teilo. Near my home is Llandaff Cathedral, known as *Teulu Teilo* (Teilo's family). It is a privilege to go there often, to be aware of all those who have gone to honour Teilo at his shrine—a great place of pilgrimage in medieval times—and to ask for his prayers for our land. It will be obvious that, for me at least, Welshness is inextricably bound up with the Christian religion. It is, I think, no accident that decline in influence of the Church—with the attendant lapse of many of our contemporaries into hedonistic paganism—has been contemporaneous with the decline of the language. National identity is expressed, yes, through language, but it is ennobled by religion. God wants the Welsh people to offer the whole of themselves to Him, and that includes the offering up of such distinctive features as their language. It is a great joy to celebrate the Eucharist in Welsh both in the Chapel of St. Michael's College, Llandaff, where I now serve, and also in the cathedral here. Here truly, at the heart of the Church's life, where mere bread and wine become truly the Body and Blood of Christ, is the affirmation of a universal fellowship but one that gathers up into itself the uniqueness of each nation, of each individual. Gwenallt saw this clearly enough when on his return to the Faith he wrote of Wales:

> Gorwedd llwch holl saint yr oesoedd
> a'r merthyron yn dy gôl
> ti a roddaist iddynt anadl
> a chymeraist hi yn ôl.

> (The dust of all the saints of the ages
> And of the martyrs lie in your bosom
> It is you who gave them breath
> And who took it back again.)

It is the same motivation that has led a man like Father Deiniol of Blaenau Ffestiniog to produce a recording of the Orthodox Liturgy in Welsh—and what a beautiful and stirring act of worship that is too!

(c) The richness of the Welsh literary tradition
In days of yore schoolchildren used to be set examination questions which began with such words as 'Compare and contrast'. The assumption

was that only when you had come across a variety of phenomena would you be able to assess the value of the individual phenomenon. So with literature, we can appreciate Shakespeare by contrasting him and his work with Ben Johnson. If that applies in English literature, it assuredly applies as between literature in different languages. Welsh literature is a fascinating field of study and re-creation. Over the last few years I have enjoyed Gwenallt, singing William Williams' hymns, mulling over Ann Griffiths' mysticism, laughing with T. Rowland Hughes' characters in *O Law i Law*, and admiring the polished prose of R. Tudur Jones in *Ffydd ac Argyfwng Cenedl*. And there is so much more too . . .

All this may seem somewhat highbrow for some people but, in truth, the appreciation of a nation's literature is a way into its shared memories.

Hitherto I have written about how my sense of Welshness was transformed on my learning the language. Yet I am very much aware that I now belong to a distinct minority even within Wales. That sometimes depresses me but, having said that, I rejoice at the enthusiasm shown by so many. Rootlessness is a curse; it leaves people with a confused sense of personal identity and impoverishes their responses to their circumstances. May this little article (about one who has returned to his roots) encourage others to esteem their homeland and to love the Christian Faith which has for long centuries moulded the character of our people. The words of the hymn sum it up:

> *Boed sain clodforedd ym mhob iaith*
> May the sound of God's praise be sung in every tongue—

and for centuries to come in the noble cadences of our Welsh language!

'SO WHAT'S ALL THE FUSS ABOUT ...?'
Lena Rhys

How can you discover what you have always known existed? We all know that certain things have got certain characteristics and attributes, so that when I first heard of Wales I knew that if there was a Wales, there would inevitably be 'Welshness', as distinct from any other kind of 'nation-ness'. Similarly, since Peru exists, there must be such a thing as 'Peruvian-ness' to make the people of that place distinct from the people of any other place, although I have no first-hand experience of it. But the real discovery occurred when I came to Wales, and realised that my assumption was not shared by everybody else.

I grew up in a small nation, and therefore see the world with the eyes of one socialised into a minority culture—not that I ever thought of it like that! I am Danish by birth, born in Copenhagen where I grew up, went to school and college, and where I—but for a chance meeting with a Welshman back in the 1960s—would very likely have spent the rest of my life. But fate plays these little tricks, and at twenty-two years of age I found myself with a Welsh husband living in a place that was an enigma to me—and twenty-two years later still from time to time remains an enigma.

I arrived here expecting to find another small European nation; although one which was politically different from what I was used to, in the sense that Wales, unlike my native country, is not a nation-state. But it seems to me that this is only important up to a point. It does not negate what sets a people apart from any other people.

What I did find was a people too overwhelmed by their neighbour to have faith in the value of their own culture and language. I was shocked, disappointed and a little contemptuous. I could have been tempted then to define 'Welshness' as cowardice, lack of backbone, as indeed it has been defined from time to time over the centuries. The enigma remains that although there is some truth in this definition, the nation has survived.

Many things have changed over the last twenty years; there is in Wales a growing awareness of nationhood in all the many and varied meanings of that word. Undoubtedly I have also changed and come to see many things differently with increased knowledge, and 'Welshness' has taken on a much more positive meaning.

I am often asked about aspects of life in Denmark, and the question always makes me feel uneasy. Apart from the most basic statements, anything I say can only be a subjective opinion with which other Danes might well disagree. I feel equally uneasy when asked to define Welshness for the same reason, and also because all too often when trying to do so the norm used is Englishness. Wales is seen as 'strange' simply because it is different from England, while it is forgotten that every single people in the world is different from every other one and that however tempting it is to see what we ourselves are used to as the norm, in reality no such norm exists.

It is very tempting to succumb to stereotypes. We have all heard about singing miners, strong, silent mountain-types, and strange, mysterious goings-on shrouded in Celtic mist, just as the aspects that come to mind all too often are of things of the past and not of the present. Wales is not a nostalgic place still living in the last century. People in Wales by and large live and earn their living in very much the same way as other people all over Europe. The Welsh language is not just the language of preaching and hymn singing. It is used in business, in teaching at all levels, as a means of everyday human interaction and communication; it is the language of the media in Wales, of television and the press. Every morning when I arrive at the office and switch on my computer I am greeted by a screen of instructions in Welsh for booting-up.

The existence of the language is undoubtedly one aspect which for many outsiders sets Wales apart, and it is tempting to think of Welshness as pertaining to Welsh speakers only. It cannot be denied that since so much of the Welsh culture is embodied in the language only Welsh speakers can be said to have any real part in that culture, but that would be far too simplistic. A large proportion of people born in Wales to parents also born and bred here have, by accident of history, aided by an English-oriented education system, lost the language, but they are and they feel just as Welsh for all that. Many try to learn the language as adults and Welsh-medium education for children from English-speaking homes has grown tremendously over the last decades, fanned by an enthusiasm for the language not always found among 'natural' Welsh speakers.

When I arrived in Wales I never for a moment doubted that I would learn the language—as indeed I have done. My first encounter with Welsh was a record of Ryan Davies singing *penillion*; a very skilful, well-articulated performance. At the time it did not (how dare I admit it?) strike me as particularly beautiful. After my arrival here I was fortunate to come into close contact with the language during frequent stays in the *Urdd Gwersyll*[1] at Llangrannog and the one at Glan-llyn. My memory of

[1] The summer camp of the Welsh League of Youth.

the experience is hearing long chains of sound and not being able to separate the chain into individual words, let alone understand what was being said. The fact that these exclusively Welsh-speaking enclaves are almost unique, was totally lost on me. Coming from a monolingual country I simply assumed that people spoke Welsh because we were in Wales and that all I could do was to learn in a hurry. Pity I was mistaken! Had I been right, Wales would have fewer problems to contend with, and I would have learned Welsh rather faster than I actually did.

I am no stranger to learning languages. During my years in school I learned English, German, French and a bit of Latin, as did everybody else, in addition to our fellow Scandinavian languages, Swedish and Norwegian, which are approximately as different from each other and from Danish as are North and South Walian from each other, but then the Europeans (aren't Wales and Britain a part of Europe, by the way?) are so good at languages. What rubbish! We are good at learning languages because we have to be. Danish as a language is of precious little use outside Denmark. However, that has never induced anybody to suggest that we should stop teaching it and make sure everybody speaks English. There are two main reasons: firstly, English is not enough— this always seems to surprise English speakers, but in a continental context it really is true. The lack of knowledge of other major European languages precludes the possibility of any sound understanding of Europe. To quote a secondary schoolteacher of mine, 'No one can claim to be cultured if unable to read Goethe in German, Molière in French, and Shakespeare in English'; the second reason is simply that it would be unthinkable: no nation worth its salt would consider such a suggestion!

My experience of learning Welsh was not a totally happy one. If I compare it to my experience of learning English there is one major difference: there was never anything emotional about attempting to learn English, no one suggested that mastering it would somehow miraculously make me English, nor that by speaking it I would become a better, more virtuous person. Having mastered it, it attracts no other comment than the occasional compliment for fluency. It was simply a matter of acquiring a means of communication. For me as an individual it would have been far easier if I could have tackled Welsh in a similar manner. Finding myself in Wales, I wanted to learn the language for purely selfish reasons: to make my own life easier. I did not learn Welsh for the sake of the language; neither would I advise anyone else to do so, but rather point out that to come to live amongst a people and not integrate to the extent of respecting the customs and learning the language is the height of crassness.

97

So Welshness is not to do with the past. It is not about ladies in tall hats; it is not even about the language. It is about having a specific outlook on life, a set of values and a distinct moral code.

To outline what exactly these attitudes are is no simple matter. It must be remembered that individuals within the society differ and what we are talking about is a predominance of particular values, not characteristics possessed by every single member of society.

If I were to choose one Welsh characteristic above all others, it would be non-aggression. Of course, I can readily think of many Welsh people who are far from being non-aggressive, but it seems to me to be one character trait shared by most of those who could be called the fathers (and mothers) of modern Wales, maybe linked to the long and honourable tradition of pacifism, especially in Welsh-speaking, chapel-going circles. There is a quietly spoken way of expression which, to me, seems particularly Welsh and which is often mistaken for weakness or compliance by those who do not understand it.

Hospitality is often mentioned as a Welsh virtue, but then no people would like to think of themselves as being inhospitable, would they? These days the subject is becoming linked with attitudes to incomers, particularly English in-migrants to Wales, and most often in a north Walian context. It must, I think, be remembered that the basic structure of the communities in north and south Wales is different. They can both be divided into Welsh-speaking and non-Welsh-speaking components, but whereas the latter in the north tends to comprise recent immigrants, it is a part of the indigenous population in the south. Personally I have found a far greater openness and a far readier welcome in south Wales than I have in north Wales (and I have lived in both areas), but I have also heard far harsher comments against Englishness and the adoption of 'English attitudes' in the south, expressed far more plainly—and through the medium of English—than anything I have ever heard said by anyone in the north.

We may also look to the arts for an expression of 'the spirit of Wales'. Traditionally artistic expression in Wales has been through the word, spoken or written. Wales possesses a rich medieval literature, and looking at the links between the Arthurian legends in Wales and on the Continent may well give an indication of how Wales has not always been on the 'fringes of Europe' as it is now. Poetry, in strict and in free metre, thrives side by side with modern prose, some of it very good and deserving of a greater audience. It is probably true to say that people in Wales read more poetry than people in most other countries and, relative to the size of population, literature and theatre are thriving. Singing is held in great esteem. 'Thank God,' as Dylan Thomas said, 'we are a musical nation!' However, the proportion of world-class singers with a Welsh background is not particularly high, nor has Wales produced many world-class composers or musicians.

Wales and Welshness are said to be in great peril. Statistics bear this out and cannot but depress one. The language is in decline, there is unlimited, unplanned immigration, which must, by definition, lead to a 'watering down' of Welshness. It is all too easy to see a bleak future.

On the other hand it is now more than 400 years since Henry VIII promised to eliminate the Welsh language, as have numerous others since then—for the benefit of the Welsh, of course! They have succeeded in inflicting damage but they have not succeeded in their ultimate goal: Wales and the Welsh language still exist. As the twentieth century draws to a close there are great changes about to happen. No country or area in Europe will be the same after 1992, and neither will Wales. What we call 'Welshness' will be changed, as all living things are changed, by outside influences. If it were not able to change, it would already be dead, and fossilised Welshness is no good for anything except as a museum exhibit. Mayby this will also bring out a much needed addition to the list of Welsh characteristics: that of self-confidence.

WELSH WINDS
Ben Ridler

I have a habit, almost instinctive by now, of converting every philosophical question of a tricky nature into its opposite. Supposing—I ask myself in trying to find out what 'Welshness' I can truly claim to have 'discovered'—supposing I were born a Welshman and came to live in England, and not the reverse, what 'Englishness' would I be discovering, inside or outside of myself? I am lucky enough to have been brought up in Oxford, a university city with historic associations for generations of Welshmen, and many have made that journey which I am making in reverse, so to speak, and written fully of the complex feelings it engenders. The great educationalist Sir Owen M. Edwards, 1858-1920, native of Llanuwchllyn in Meirionnydd and scholar of Balliol College, Oxford is one interesting example. But what of the essence?

Comparisons of coolness, detachment, on the English side, with a more instinctive, even 'feminine' consciousness, on the Welsh side, begin to form in my mind. But these are indeed tricky concepts to pin down. Is not this at some point the dilemma of every thinking human being? Goethe well knew that pinning a butterfly down is a wonderful way of studying something which, *in essence*, is no longer truly a butterfly. Am I already applying my trained English mind to analysing away a mystery most Welshmen would not want to disturb? (Teasingly, I hear mocking me the final words of Robert Graves' famous 'Walk at Criccieth', when the listeners, fretting for more wonders or explanations of wonders, are told—'I was *coming* to that!' And the suspense remains.) But for me, the essence finally comes down to an experience of *time*.

True, I am living in rural Wales, and to some extent there is always a change of rhythm to be felt when moving from an urban to a more rural lifestyle. But I believe the experience goes further than that. The Reverend Eli Jenkins' sunset poem, with its invocation of mountains and rivers is, of course, partly caricature. Nonetheless, it is inspired by the gab of birds and the presence of 'the eternal hills'. And my personal experience since living in Wales is of a life more generally lived, however imperfectly and at times infuriatingly, in awareness of the rhythms of nature and, more fundamentally, the perspective of eternity.

Anecdotal evidence will speak louder than theory. I remember making a joke in my first supply job in Wales, teaching English in the secondary school in Blaenau Ffestiniog before a large class of (then) 'O'-level pupils, many of them girls—and feeling it go horribly wrong. I forget the joke, or non-joke, but I know I felt over-sophisticated, 'racy', in a way I did not like. Timing, in jokes or elsewhere, is not always—in fact very rarely—a matter of calculation. I felt out of touch. The collective will of the class—in this instance!—seemed healthier.

I remember 'Griff', the pensioner who after the war laid the tiles in the cottage where I now live, making a reply which also made me feel over-speedy. Griff is distinguished for his headgear, usually bowler, ex-army beret, or Tyrolean hat with a flower, and rides a tricycle. He rode it proudly in the town carnival a few years ago, bearing behind his saddle the label 'Chariots of Fire'. Having found out just previously that he was responsible for the excellent tiled floor, I invited him—in the month of October—to come up and look at it once more. 'I'll come in the spring,' he said. What confidence! What certainty! (I am happy to say he has lived many springs since then.) I realised with a shock that although half his age, and so with theoretically twice his life-prospects, I certainly had more than twice his doubts.

I remember also a formative experience working for a summer and autumn on a major local construction-scheme, building a by-pass. Many of the workmen were Welsh, although not all. Certainly the work took place in the shadow and presence of some eternal Welsh hills, and we were blasting, humping, hefting and heaving what seemed doggedly eternal rock. 'Lift, man, lift,' I was told as I raised my pick, 'and the good Lord will let it fall.' Jock it was—a Scotsman, in fact—who gave me the best advice of all. It was the quiet, measured confidence of his manner, as much as his words, that rang home. 'Just take it one step at a time.' Not for nothing has Trebor Edwards' record *'Un Dydd ar y Tro'* (One Day at a Time), become one of the most popular Welsh-made records.

There are times when this somewhat more relaxed attitude to time has its negative aspects. I am by no means totally ashamed of my 'English' (if such it be) impatience to 'get things done'. Being vague as to time and place (I do not wish to use the word slippery, often applied to the Welsh) can be maddening. On the whole, however, my encounter with a subtly different awareness of time has been positive and enhancing.

But to begin—no, not at the beginning, but in the middle, both of my life, and of this attempt to shape the elusive. For it was half a lifetime ago, from this present standpoint in time, that I first came to stay in the beautiful county of Meirionnydd, in what is now Gwynedd, north Wales. (A popular if presumptuous tale among local architects has it that God, while creating the world, spent six days on the technical drawings for Meirionnydd, and a day on the rest.) My 'discovery' is thus quintessentially of *north* Welshness. I knew Pembrokeshire from childhood holidays, but those merge in my memory with equally happy times spent in Cornwall. I have a diary of a holiday spent in Cardiganshire, staying on Dic Jones's farm; his name meant nothing to me then, but I remember being baffled by the number of armchairs in the front room, all with little silver plaques on them! I treasure the picture of my younger brother hugging Dic Jones's farm-dog. These were family experiences, no less important for that; but I associate my discovery of Meirionnydd with an awakening of my own personal consciousness. I must at once confess to never yet having met a double of R. S. Thomas's Iago Prydderch, whose dour image represented the 'typical' Welshman in my mind before this time. From the first, I found the people of Meirionnydd welcoming, tolerant, warm of heart, and willing to forgive; and so it continues to this day. Of course, in any community, particularly a small one, the range of human merit and weakness soon reveals itself; but nonetheless, those epithets still ring true to my experience.

Peter Walker, M.P., in his speech both as the then Secretary of State for Wales and as President of the Day in the 1989 Llangollen International Eisteddfod, referred to the 'spirit of community' as the single most unifying feature linking the Welsh of the industrial Valleys with the Welsh of rural Wales. That view validates my own perception of life in rural north Wales, observed in one 'constellation' of village, market- and county-town—respectively, Llanfachreth, Dolgellau, Caernarfon. For all the dangers of provincialism inherent in such smallness of scale, I find the resulting intimacy and clarity of the social process refreshing, especially after an upbringing in large cities with their more anonymous profile. The columns of the *Cambrian News*, very rarely troubled by news of cataclysmic impact, continue to make compulsive weekly reading.

Specifically, one moment, one word almost, summarises a discovery which later led to the gradual attempt to make the painful transition from 'townie' to country-dweller. I remember emerging from the car after being fetched from Machynlleth railway station—and inhaling a lungful of fresh, fresh air. It was as if I had never smelt before. The following acquaintance with birds, flowers, skies, had a similar quality of unexpectedness. Suddenly I understood—or felt I understood—what academic studies had previously failed to illumine, namely, why Shakespeare set such store by the word 'nature': why for him it mainly represented wholeness, healing, all that could bring man eventually to balance, harmony. The 'discovery' is nothing new: what mattered was to be making such a connection *for oneself*. Others have had greater revelations in Katmandu. The fact remains that one is deeply grateful for any place that can bestow such an experience.

Personal associations, whether positive or negative, with particular places, are ultimately a mystery. I have visited many beautiful parts of Britain and the Continent. But even in Wales—even in north Wales— none for me provides quite the same warmth of inner affirmation as Meirionnydd. Relatively short journeys can yield the same response over and over again, on passing the border-sign marking re-entry into the old county. In the words of a Leah Owen song, *'mae'r wefr yr un o hyd'*— the thrill is the same as ever. I cannot and would not want to be able to explain why, only know that it is so.

Gratitude, resonance, re-awakening—these terms apply also to the further, immense personal discovery of the Welsh language, or truly 'Cymric' Welshness, which it would require a separate 'raid on the inarticulate' to describe. (One of the first, and wisest, Welsh sayings I learnt in Welsh, from a Welsh-speaking friend, was *'Ym mhopeth*

102

byddwch yn ddiolchgar'—not just 'for', but '*in* everything, be grateful'.) When asked by friends what I most enjoy about living in Wales, I like to reply teasingly, 'the wind'. There are exceptions, but on the whole the wind hereabouts is gentle, moulding, caressing. The language is not altogether unlike this in character. Even—or especially—those plagues of the beginner, the mutations, serve to round or mould all jagged edges of sound, creating a graceful flow. To be able to speak even a few words of Welsh provokes a show of appreciation often quite undeserved, and to begin by means of language to share some of the wisdom and humour of a community from within, so to speak, is indeed a blessing.

Welsh may or may not be 'the language of heaven', but it certainly has the power to make the soul aspire to a richer understanding of spiritual matters, to which it seems marvellously attuned.

A modest but again personally significant realisation of this fact arose, in tragic circumstances, when I tried to pay tribute to a friend who died in an accident working (as he often did) after hours to try and help meet a need. The words would not come in English. The only possible formulation of a response, however inadequate, had to be in Welsh. (Friends were on hand, as always, to correct and guide from a linguistic point of view.) Hywel Puw, or 'HP' as he was known, was an engineer-mechanic with a genius for persuading reluctant televisions to function, known as 'the Good Samaritan' for his unstinting efforts at providing a service as good for the disadvantaged as for those more fortunate. I would like therefore to dedicate my contribution to the memory of a Welshman who, in his quiet way, represented all that is best in the values of his family, his community, his country; and who taught me much about the meaning of the word integrity. He had loved and served the beautiful church of Bryncoedifor, and died just after Easter, in 1988.

Er Cof am Hywel Puw Owen

Cynhesrwydd ei wên
sy'n dal i roi fflach o liw
i'r darlun, heb fyth ei orffen,
o'r Arglwydd a garodd o.

Ond O! 'dan ni'n eiddigeddus
o feddwl ei fod, ar ei ffordd,
yn agosach na ni
i ddirgelwch y sgwrs
a gynheuodd dân yn llygaid y rhai
a welodd harddwch
y Dieithryn ar daith i Emaus.

(In memory of 'HP': the warmth of his smile still adds a flash of colour to the picture—never fully complete—of the Lord he loved.

But O!—how jealous we are at the thought that, as he goes, he's nearer than us to the secret of the words that kindled fire in the eyes of those who actually *saw* the beauty of the Stranger on his way to Emmaus.)

CYNGHANEDD
Pat Neill

'What about trying to write an *englyn*?' my very good friend the Welshman asked me.

'An *englyn*?'

'Yes. It's the most popular type of Welsh poem written nowadays. It's very short—only thirty syllables!'

Thirty syllables. Even to somebody of my limited Welsh ability, thirty syllables didn't sound extortionate. I am by nature lazy and, judging by the popularity of the *englyn*, the Welsh, or at any rate the literary aspirants of the nation, were inclined to indolence as well. If I could achieve bardic recognition by churning out say, on an average, twenty words—allowing one and a half syllables a word—then I was prepared to do the churning. An hour's work and hey bingo! there would be my passport to *Talwrn y Beirdd*.

'Of course,' continued Dewi, 'you'll have to learn a bit about *cynghanedd*.'

'*Cynghanedd*?' I was beginning to sound more like a demented parrot upon each exchange. 'Tell me more.'

'I taught English poetry, not Welsh. I couldn't give you the ins-and-outs of it, but I could get you a simple book about *cynghanedd*. Next time you pop over I'll let you have it.'

The next popping duly produced a book called in translation 'Sound of the Click'. As it was aimed towards the enlightenment of not too bright eleven-year olds, I was able, with the liberal use of a dictionary, to understand the gist of what the author had in mind. Each brief chapter took the reader one step further towards unravelling the secrets of the bards, and there were sets of exercises designed, through their simplicity, to give a warm feeling of confidence to all who had sufficient energy to raise a pen. My ninety-eight percent success rate left me floating in the proverbial rosy-coloured world of make believe. I was confident that I had joined the clique who understood the click.

There was an eisteddfod for learners looming. What better way to achieve instant fame could there be than astounding the judges with my know-how? If I searched the *Geiriadur Mawr*—the large Welsh dictionary—long enough, I should be bound to find some words whose consonants clicked together in the same order: for that basically appeared to be the secret. Looking back on that attempt five years ago I still blush at my temerity, and wonder at the mildness of the criticism directed at my chain of so-called *englynion*. Apart from breaking at least one rule on every line (for I am afraid my book for beginners avoided mentioning the traps set for the unwary) the words I had dredged from the depths of the dictionary, and which were for the most part conveniently marked by an asterisk, had died from neglect centuries before.

And there are traps so numerous and complicated that it takes a three-year course, somewhat similar to a degree course, to come to terms with them all. In the old days of bardic pride a master poet would teach his craft to an apprentice. Anyone not having such tuition would be bound to break one or more of the secret laws, and his work would be laughed out of court.

I can imagine one bearded bard nudging an equally hairy friend and saying, 'Did you spot the *proest* there? Chuck the poem on the scrap heap. And no largesse for him tonight—we can't have people like him *proest*-ing about the place and spoiling our reputation for *proest*-free products.'

And the poor fellow would have to brew up some nettle soup to stop his tummy rumbling, wondering the nonce what heinous crime he had committed. And there was no fairy godmother available to take him to one side and explain things to him. To learn the rules of *cynghanedd* he had to have the full treatment, and this usually meant a costly live-in apprenticeship. Unless he was amply endowed with the ready cash, or had very pretty blue eyes, this course of instruction would have been beyond him, and he would never have achieved acceptance as a bard.

Nowadays the secrets have been revealed, and the medieval rules relaxed a little—for example, a poet is allowed to have more than one line in a verse starting with a vowel—but there still remain sixteen classes of cardinal errors, and one slip in these still puts the whole poem at fault, even if the actual sound of the 'click' is superb.

In what, then, lies the attraction of writing *cynghanedd*? Is it that, like banging one's head against a wall, it is very pleasant when one stops? Or is it like the experience of the climber, who scales a mountain just

105

because it is there? I would suggest that it is more like the latter, though I should liken it rather to a combination of the pleasure the mathematician gains when he has solved a complicated problem and the satisfaction felt by the researcher when his diligence has opened up new avenues in his field of studies. There is, to be sure, a *soupçon* of the head-banging syndrome present as well. At times I have spent a dozen or so hours trying to write a couplet worthy of the name, and succeeded only in filling the waste-paper basket with my abortive endeavours. Yes, at those times it is very agreeable indeed to stop. But, when the birth is successful, when the idea, conceived in the first flush of activity, comes to fruition after a nightmare of labour, then the effort is forgotten in the pleasure of creation. And when one's fellow bards admire the progeny, or when it is publicly exalted through the printed page, the hours of head-banging are disregarded.

What sort of baby is it, that is produced by *cynghanedd*? Surely, constrained by so many rules and regulations, it must be a very unnatural child?

Strangely enough, what is brought forth is not an automaton. Those rules, which have been developing over the past thousand years as the Welsh language has developed, enhance the inherent music in the tongue, and produce a perfectly adjusted offspring, a natural harmony of language and artifice. But they have been developed for Welsh and Welsh alone. I have seen many attempts at writing an English *englyn*, some of them by noted composers of the Welsh version, but very few of the poems seem comfortable. They are like children who have dressed up in their parents' clothes, a parody of reality and not a joy for ever. Even the Welsh principles of rhyme do not coincide with English notions. The English poet would not even consider rhyming 'listen' with 'men', but in an *englyn* one is forced, by the rules laid down, to include such rhymes. Likewise the English are used to regular metres—iambic and trochees and the like—and it is very difficult for them to appreciate the more subtle rhythms of the seven-syllable line in which most *cynghanedd* is written. In using English examples, therefore, to introduce the reader to this art form, I am conscious of manufacturing a hybrid which is a mockery of the real thing.

I am not, in a thousand words or so, going to try to produce a crash-course in *cynghanedd*. That would be totally impossible. Instead, I am taking one type of *cynghanedd*, *Draws*, and exposing part of its skeleton so that, if you are the type who likes anatomizing poetry, you can buckle down to dissecting your first Welsh *englyn*, even if you can't understand a word of the language. And, as about three-quarters of strict metres are *Draws* or similar forms, you will have a pretty good strike rate.

We'll assume that we have a seven-syllable line—again, the most common length. The last word will be stressed—as in English it is not common to make a rhyme using an unstressed word like 'a', for example —and there will also be a stressed word about half way through the line. Take this nonsensical line:

Come to mé, O comet Márs.

I have put a stress mark over the vowel in the words 'me' and 'Mars'. Now let us look at all the consonants that come before that first stressed vowel in 'me'. They are C, M, T and M again. These four consonants in that same order must come directly before the stressed vowel in our final word:

CoMe To Mé,   o   CoMeT Márs.

As they do so, the line is *cynghanedd*-ly correct. However, 'Come to me, comet of Mars' would be faulty because the sequence before the second stressed vowel has now become C, M, T, F, M, and the 'F' did not appear in the first half.

Let us look at another line:

Are you hópping, dear híppo?

Here the accented vowel in each case is in a two-syllable word. I have answered 'hopping' by 'hippo', which I am allowed to do, as long as I include, in the *cynghanedd*, not only all the sounded consonants before the first accented vowel, but also those immediately following it.

Are you hopping (R, H, /, P), dear hippo (D, R, H, /, P).

I have done so, and therefore the line is technically perfect. Pardon? Oh, so you noticed the extra 'D'? To make things a little easier, one is allowed to include extra consonants between the first accented word and the start of the second sequence of repeated consonants.

A couple of other little remissions have been passed down through the centuries as sops to struggling bards. Firstly, one can ignore the letter 'h' completely. No doubt Dafydd ap Gwilym or someone similar dropped his aitches, and this rule was invented so as not to embarrass him.

107

Secondly, one can use an 'n' before any other consonants appear and that also can be disregarded. Perhaps the poor fellow was suffering from adenoids as well. A line such as:

Now the cráb is up the créek   (N, Th, C, R, /, (SP) Th, C, R, /)

is permissible because one can ignore the first 'n'. The 'w' in 'now' is here a vowel (as are all 'w''s in Welsh) so that doesn't count as a consonant either. Easy, is'nt it? Well, you just try writing a line, and I'll have a look at it when I've finished.

You must remember that I have dealt with only part of one type of *cynghanedd*, sufficient, I hope, for you to appreciate some of the intricacies of this art form. To try to do more would cause confusion: in fact you might have noticed a few iotas of perplexity jostling around already. Three or four months ago an English poet asked me to teach him enough basic *cynghanedd* for him to write an English *englyn*: he thought three lessons might suffice, as he would put all the information on his computer. After the second of the two-hour sessions his computer malfunctioned, and the third lesson left him in such a state of shock that the mere mention of the word '*englyn*' still causes convulsions. And even then I had attempted to explain only five of the fifteen-odd types of *cynghanedd*, and had skirted very lightly over just the two most important traps for the unwary. As I said somewhere about the four-hundred and seventy-fifth word, the acquisition of comprehensive *cynghanedd*-ology is a mammoth task.

Why then have I persevered for the past five years? Mostly, I believe, because, combined with my laziness, there is an even more influential stubborn streak. After my farcical effort in the Learners' Eisteddfod my Welsh teacher took me to one side and advised me to forget *cynghanedd* —she had tried to write *englynion* herself and been unsuccessful, so what, in Heaven's name, did I think I could achieve? I can still feel my lips whitening at the challenge: there was the mountain; was I going to duck climbing it? I dug my metaphorical heels in and started the uphill struggle.

Now I have reached the top of several peaks, only to find that there is an even higher one to scale. The highest peak of all is the chair presented at the National Eisteddfod. I shall try for it, of course—my stubborn streak will see to that. Recently one of my friends, Idris Reynolds, who with me attended the *cynghanedd* classes run by the late Dr Roy Stephens, won the chair, but he, of course, had the advantage of being Welsh born and bred. For me in my dotage, and with less than a decade of Welsh to bolster my effort, the task is almost impossible. It is that 'almost' that I cling to: instant fame could still be mine!

You think you might like to master the *englyn*? If so, find classes to attend. You'll have to learn Welsh first, of course, but that is the easier part of the challenge. Stick to it, and by the year 2000 you might be contesting the National Eisteddfod chair yourself.

Did you manage to complete that line of *cynghanedd*? Fine. Let's have a look at it.

'Aunt Sally is not solo.' Well, the accent is on the 'a' of 'Sally' and the 'o' of 'solo' so we have:

N, T, S,/, L in the first half and S, N, T, S,/, L in the second. We can disregard the 's' before the second group, leaving us with the same group of consonants in each half. By the way, the two 'l''s in Sally only count as one, so don't worry about that.

'Is it perfect *cynghanedd*?' you ask. Oh dear, oh dearie me, please excuse me for chuckling, but I'm afraid you've gone and *proest*-ed. The line's worthless, absolutely worthless. I hope you don't mind my saying this, dear reader, but don't you think you'd better stick to your Welsh classes and forget about trying to write *cynghanedd*?

ON TRANSLATING WELSH POETRY
(Cywydd)

Tony Conran

(The 'Bedwyr' mentioned is one of the friends of the poet to whose help
he makes acknowledgement in his book.)

Bedwyr, this frantic burden
Severs wholly me from men.
It's what makes me not notice
The too much time that I miss.
So hard—the hazard is huge
I deal against a deluge
While a dotty world yet wags
Trumps from its thousand handbags!—
Tomorrow and tomorrow,
Each day's a leech, lays me low:
So hard, to string in English
The tied Welsh that I would wish
And scan without cynghanedd,
Heart's clamour, labour of lathe,
Hammer-stroke—how I'm stricken!—
To give, I'm at it again,
A mirror of its merit
To the cywydd wild with wit.

WHY I WRITE IN WELSH
Bobi Jones

I write English like a dead language. This is probably will-power.

When I write Welsh, however, it is not by choice. There is nothing voluntary about that medium. Confronted with the muse, I find that it (to adopt the usual cliché) stuffs the Welsh language down my throat.

Language is so totalitarian. How else would many of the most interesting writers in Greek, Hebrew, Latin and Sanskrit have *chosen* to write in a second language, even in a 'dead' language? I suspect that Beckett in his second language, like Conrad in his third, experienced this same compulsion to discovery and *chose* the path of least resistance.

I am not the first to notice this totalitarianism. When imperialist England submerged Wales, the first and last blow at destruction was at the language. Conquer that, and conquer all. A Welshman might henceforth feel a superficial equality in other spheres, but regarding his own country he was permanently condemned. Even inferiority in the economy would now be accepted because the language had inferior status. This was the norm for centuries, the mentality of slant towards London. The language was to be the economy, was politics, was industry, was science: when the language rolled over, they all rolled over.

The key to our dull dark cell was found a long time ago; but the door was not properly opened until about 1936. And Welsh men very slowly and hesitantly, some fearfully, even terrified, began to creep out into the open air: many still cowered in the cupboard. Others slept.

The same thing has been happening over most of the world. Those inbreeding, monoglot, parochial people next door are amazed when they visit the five continents and discover the incomprehensible people everywhere who have been excited by their roots. Why don't they grow up and speak English? Why not die 'internationalists'?

Suddenly, everywhere, we are no longer foreigners standing before our own past. We belong to our land, and are responsible, psychologically and culturally responsible for it before the whole world.

To be born into this is naturally an inspiring experience, as it involves one in the greatest constructive cultural movement on this globe in this century. In scores of countries there has been a strong affirmation. It is true that there are here and there some very important areas of decadence; but culturally or socially, there has been in many places a positive bid for life. This cultural and psychological movement is something we

111

are very conscious of in Wales, and it is paralleled with a movement towards or into the language.

This affirmation has been my main artistic interest, and its linking through and within the Welsh language in my work is a part of its character. The affirmation, naturally, has reservations: all of us who recognise original sin as an axle point in the human predicament can understand that empty optimism about the language and the universal civilisation it symbolises and enshrines would be pointless. The dangers for the language are a part of the dangers of living in the last decade of the twentieth century. But in moving away from the decadence of our culture towards a renewed vigour, one finds that the old-fashioned Anglo-Welsh masochism, for instance, peels off, and Wales is no longer just a sordid boghouse at the bottom of a coal-tip. Welsh history is no longer just depression. Gradually, the inferiority we felt about Welsh nationhood and identity no longer exists, and the language can wash over the sores. Gradually, the immense parochialism of the 'Englishman', with his negation of all that the world stands for, is replaced by a realisation of the essential variety within the unity.

As a dogmatic Calvinist, the accidents of life never seem very convincing to me. In my own personal history, there may appear, on the surface, to be an element of the accidental, and my first real encounter with the Welsh language was all just an unfortunate mistake, and should not properly have happened. So too, I suspect with the whole society. No doubt those neutralist historians, who discuss history as a series of undirected events, could make out a solid case for this absolutely incongruous movement towards the language as being just an understandable disturbance in the genes of the community. But I would plump for election.

We were a shy band, on a September morning in 1940, standing before a grand old gentleman from Lancashire, Mr J. O. Cheetham. It was his lot to divide us into three streams, two to take Spanish, one to take Welsh. French was—well, compulsory is not the word—a 'natural' subject, like English and the air we breathed.

There were ninety of us, and he asked those who wished to 'do' Welsh to stand forward. Some five quivering schoolboys ventured a step. The rest of us stood our ground, certain that Spanish would be intensely useful for our commercial weekend trips to South America later on. And would we not have chosen Timbuktuish, if such a language existed, rather than degrade ourselves to do that indeed-to-goodness stuff?

But the headmaster had his job to do, and needed a 'stream': at a push, twenty-five might do, but certainly not five. It was war-time, and

112

volunteering was in the air. 'Tell me, my boy,' said he, turning on a fat blushing specimen in the middle of the front row, 'why don't you want to do Welsh?'

'I know enough, sir'.

Had I not done it in the elementary?

'Well, tell me, my boy. What's "good morning" in Welsh?'

This was one of those phrases that had somehow slipped the syllabus of the elementary. The blush reached my knees.

'Tell me, my boy. What's "good night"?'

This too had slipped attention. The blush rattled to the floor.

'Don't you think you'd better reconsider your decision?'

The vision had come.

I was converted. On that sad September day my fate was sealed, and unknown to myself I now slid into the clutches of one who must be amongst the most brilliant Welsh teachers Wales has ever employed— W. C. Elvet Thomas. Quite by accident, of course.

The rot set in.

It is impossible for me to analyse the quality of his teaching, but I have always supposed that the main secret of his gift was that he used the language as an introduction to the whole versatility and contemporary energy of Wales. Language was not just a means of communication, and certainly not a school subject. It was the expression of a complete national life and was linked to place-names, the *Urdd*, mountains and history, poetry and songs, dances and drama and the eisteddfod, altars, and lots of enthralling Welsh characters and anecdotes.

My ambitions were, naturally, in Africa at the time. And so they continued into my first year in college. I had, at the bright shining age of nine, decided to be a missionary, and kept my path direct all the way to the university: I thought that I could conveniently shed my Welsh after the first college session, and raise my sights to broader horizons.

However, another collision with the parish-pump occurred during the first term. This accident was in the shape of inspiring university teachers and a new type of ethos amongst Welsh-speaking students never before encountered. Even at that advanced stage in my education, although fully able to read Welsh, and write it less fluently, I was completely socially dumb, due to the artificial examination emphasis on written answers. Now, for the first time, I came into contact with the rollicking charm of the *gwerin*. A tidy anglophile from Cardiff became immersed in the warmth and gaiety of a rural culture hitherto hidden from him, in the form of students, and in a teacher who was as intense about the Latin element in Welsh as if it were the Day of Judgement.

113

And it was my day of no return, to say the least.

For an adolescent involved in such a personal upheaval, there had to be a most disconcerting reorientation.

Dreaming in Welsh, lovemaking in Welsh, poems, stories, children, friends, a nation, the whole world: the relationship between peoples, this daily consciousness of international friction and its dangerous but golden possibilities, from the inside, no longer dead or academic or up in the gallery, but here down in the arena. Writing in Welsh means now to be in the middle of the great human struggle—not to have pulled out, not to be superior or neutral or to have one's eyes on the ends of the world as if they were not here; it is to be sensitive to the tingling life of words, to the rhythmic muscles of sentences, to the quiveringness of images, to the possession of great themes. It is to turn the soil in this part of the earth as it should really be turned.

For a middle-aged man I presume there must be a settling down too, although to settle down in the Welsh language today is rather like trying to snatch a nap on the tip of a volcano. But by now, for me, there are so many more cogent reasons for writing in Welsh: quiet ones, old ones, long ones. Welsh has been for many years my first language, and practically speaking, my only language. There is so little time to read any other languages, as the Welsh materials are endless and so tremendously versatile; they are the windows of the whole world. Writing in English or any other foreign language is, for me, a discipline, necessary but almost tedious and irrelevant. I still can't help savouring the salty tang of a Welsh which will always be for me a new-old language. My ancient dynamite.

In his delightful essays, *The Dragon has Two Tongues*, Glyn Jones refers to himself as belonging to a generation or rather a series of generations that had moved away from the Welsh language, or as he says, 'From Taf Carmarthenshire to Taf Glamorganshire, in fact'. A few years previously I had brought out a little book of verse *Rhwng Taf a Thaf* (Between Taf and Taf), referring to the same two rivers but expressing a completely contrary experience. I suppose I belong to the opposite generation, maybe generations, younger than Glyn Jones; but would agree whole-heartedly with him that a writer's 'mother' tongue, in the literal sense, is not necessarily his best medium for his creative work—but 'the language which captures his heart and imagination during the emotional and intellectual upheavals of adolescence, the language of his awakening, the language in which ideas—political, religious, aesthetic—and an understanding of personal and social relationships first dawn upon his mind'. This is the language that writes him.

'Rhaid i'r Iaith Fyw!' by Suzanne Greenslade

During each of the last three centuries, it is worth noting that there has been at least one poet in Wales creating in his second language who must be accounted amongst the two or three greatest poets of his age, namely Iolo Morganwg, Islwyn and Waldo Williams. They have written in the language of their hearts. For me, in a much more minor way, the same has again been true. Why I write Welsh is partly why I write at all: there is no longer any question to answer.

THE WELSH LANGUAGE
Bobi Jones

I

She has the cement that joins us as a people again.
The foundations are hers, and beneath her the drains of our blood
Run through her underground mystery. The rocks have been raised
In order, a dwelling-place for us: the past possessed
Is a door to our fair present. Let us walk inside
And own what she owns. Since hers is the strongest
Cement ever: let us boldly live within her
Against all stormy weathers . . . We need only pay the rent.
The rent must be paid. But pay? Good Lord!
For a bed whose match was never spread beneath any sea,
For music, benches on all sides, songs of every savour,
For bread hot from the Lord God's oven!
Pay! Fool! Had we all the lives in Creation,
We could not pay one-hundredth of the grief of bearing her obliteration.

II

Delicate her columns of breath, finely wrought!
They rise up high from their fair foundations,
Yet a crowd runs from her, their hands screaming aloft,
Her air foul to their ears and vomit to their mouths.
Some try like a mole to hold her on their shoulders, fearing
Her fall every second. But no one is able
To escape her. She is like life that closes
Widely around us. It's pointless for the servile
To seek another hearth: she's completely the world
And every pain is her pain, every weakness her weakness.
She is a temple where generations gather: in her
The prayers and the praise that can heal burn incense.
Oh! language that stood in the teeth of centuries of storm like a miracle
On the slopes of worn mountains, take us into your gates.

Bobi Jones
trans. Joseph P. Clancy

FOREIGNERS
John Barnie

In the television series *'Allo 'Allo*, the main characters speak English with heavy 'French' and 'German' accents; it's part of the comedy. However, in England even straight drama represents foreigners in this way, to such an extent that the English have become adept at identifying Spaniards, Italians, Greeks, Swedes, Russians, Chinese, Indians, Arabs, Jews, by conventions of accent, grammatical error and malapropisms in their spoken English. A recent television drama had Hitler speaking with a 'German' accent.

All nations have stereotypes of other nations with whom they are in contact, but the English have invented 'foreigners' in a thorough and perhaps unique way. The reason for this—the dominance of English as a world *lingua franca*—is clear enough. Its psychological and cultural effects, however, are not so clear, especially to the English themselves.

One is that because they are so used to hearing foreigners speak English with varying degrees of inaccuracy, the English find it hard to take people from other language cultures seriously. Their perception of them is refracted by the distorting medium of English, in which a foreigner is likely to feel restricted, but the Englishman not. It is unusual for an Englishman to have the opposite experience—trying to converse in another language and coming up against limits of expression, while the native speaker, the 'foreigner', is fluent and at ease. On the whole, few English people feel the need to get up a second language.

The stature of English as a world language also facilitates a sense, for the native speaker, of the boundlessness of what can be expressed in it. This leads to an easy and unreflecting reliance on translation. Should a writer from another language come into prominence in the English-speaking world, it will be through translation. Few would think of learning Spanish to read Gabriel García Márquez, for example. If Márquez brings out a new novel, it is natural to wait for the translation, which 'becomes' the novel, for all practical purposes, in the English consciousness.

In so far as such attitudes are shared by members of other territorial nations in the United Kingdom—the Scots, the Welsh, the Northern Irish—they are also central to the definition of the term 'British'. The anglicization of Wales can almost be monitored by the progress of such dominant English attitudes towards the language.

I was British in this sense, brought up in the highly anglicized border town of Abergavenny in the 1940s and 1950s. Though I belonged to the third generation of my family to live in Gwent, my father or mother would say, scornfully, 'You're not Welsh', if the question of identity was raised. And of course it was true. At school my English master introduced us to Dylan Thomas and R. S. Thomas, but for the rest, in a way quite rightly, we studied the classics of English literature. In history, I studied the history of the British Empire at 'O' level; modern English and European history at Advanced. There was also a minor in Welsh history, which I passed without having perceived, because I was never told, that the Welsh language was in any way fundamental to the Methodist Revival.

The only Welsh I heard was on the radio—programmes that seemed to come from a long way away. There was no encouragement to learn the language. It was a barrier to communication. 'What do they want to speak it for?' my father would say. 'They all speak English.'

Everyone spoke English. It was natural. I studied French to 'O' level but it was taught like Latin, as if it were a dead language. We never heard anyone speak it fluently except the French master, and I believe I had only the vaguest notion that it was a language in which people could feel and see, and be themselves, as I could in English.

It was only as a postgraduate student that I began to take an interest in languages, learning Old Icelandic and Spanish because I wanted to read more of the literature, and Medieval Latin and Anglo-Norman French because they were necessary for my work. These were languages on the page, set apart, which I could attend to as an exciting puzzle. Except for Spanish, I had largely imagined their pronunciation, and when I heard Icelandic spoken in Denmark, I was disappointed—it had a far narrower range of tone than I expected.

Such a passive knowledge limited the impact of languages on me. However, in 1969 I went to live in Denmark and stayed there for thirteen years. Before I left England I started to teach myself Danish from a grammar, much as I'd learned Old French. But when I arrived, I found this preparation next to useless. The language was so slippery on the tongues of the Danes. My carefully assembled grammatical structures and rehearsed phrases left me suddenly and frustratingly dumb.

I went to an evening class but gave it up. I found I preferred listening to people, internalizing words, phrases, rhythms to use as I became familiar with them. But as my Danish improved, I had the common experience that speaking another language alters the 'I' that is being expressed. I had not realized before that what you are is partly formed by what you speak. I had also not understood how culture and language are inseparable, and how both are bound up in the expression of individuality. It is certainly possible to have a good knowledge of a language in terms of its grammar, syntax, vocabularly, and to be a fluent speaker at a rather abstracted level; but if you have not internalized the minutiae of the culture, the expression of self in that language will be thin. On the other hand, the nearer you get to a grasp of the cultural dimension of a language, the more that language refracts your identity as you speak it.

Thinking about these things, I began to think, too, that my sense of Wales must have been refracted by the English I was brought up with in the shadow of the Black Mountains. Becoming more active in Danish, looking out as it were from another window, I began to wonder what it would be like seeing Wales through the medium of Welsh.

To try to find out, I started learning Welsh from Caradar's *Welsh Made Easy* (still the best comprehensive grammar I've come across) and after a while began working through the stories of Kate Roberts, D. J. Williams and others. What this gave me was a first glimpse of Wales as a different territory, transformed by the language which perceived and created it. The 'Wales' I had grown up with and felt deeply about, I had to learn was an English overlay which had made me feel secure at the cost of making me British and the Welsh 'foreign'.

There was no one to speak Welsh with in Copenhagen and so my knowledge remained passive. But I continued reading—Saunders Lewis, Gwenallt, T. H. Parry-Williams, Waldo Williams. At the same time I was reading their contemporaries in Anglo-Welsh literature, many of them for the first time. If the 'Anglo-Welsh' theory is correct, I should have had the experience of reading a national Welsh literature in my own language. But I didn't. Instead I had a general sense of a provincial literature in which whatever the surface manifestations of 'Welshness' might be, powerful currents of language and cultural influence pulled poems and stories into the sea of English literature. Reading Anglo-Welsh literature of the 1980s confirms this.

Some believe there is more than one Wales—Wales of the Valleys, Pembrokeshire, the Black Mountains. There is enough truth in this to give the notion a plausible veneer. But while English may have mediated for a while, in the inter-war years, between Welsh-language culture on one side and English high art and mass culture on the other—especially in the Valleys—that balance was essentially delicate. Any major economic change or population movement could tip it very quickly to the advantage of English culture and a British outlook. Welsh-language culture is threatened, of course, by the same forces, but there is a determinant, the language, which makes it possible to see more clearly what is happening and where one must stand.

In 1982 I returned to Abergavenny, and in 1985 moved to Aberystwyth to work on the magazine *Planet*. For the first time, I had the chance to speak Welsh to people in ordinary social contexts. After five years I still speak it poorly, but it took ten years to get any command of Danish as I am a slow learner. It's impossible with my background ever to 'become' Welsh as I now understand the term. Thirteen years in Denmark taught me that, for most, the language you are brought up in is the water in which you must swim. Only a few people are capable of making the imaginative shift of a Bobi Jones.

Yet Danish, the language of a small, buoyant nation, led me to Welsh. Together they have given me a perception of Wales and myself which, however much I change, I can never shrug off.

RHIANNON, MABON AND ME
Noragh Jones

'Lady,' asks Pwyll of Rhiannon in the *Mabinogi*, 'where are you coming from and where are you going?' It is the question asked of strangers in Celtic vision tales, and is still asked today (though not so openly) when the stranger arrives in a rural Welsh community. 'I go my own errands,' replies Rhiannon the liberated. It turns out she has chosen Pwyll for her man and Dyfed for her country, and only if rejected will she go elsewhere. Any kind of lasting commitment has to be a dialogue. When you come to live in another country (or even another community in your own country) both you and your hosts are vulnerable till (like travellers of old) you find a tale to tell that earns you a seat near the fire and the right to hear the true tales of your new country. Welshness is a process not a product, a relationship not an acquisition.

I came from Ireland (via England) to live in Ceredigion seven years ago, with Ken who is of Liverpool-Welsh descent. We had known Wales from the outside through many years of visiting its historic places and walking in the hills of mid and north Wales. Since then each of us has been finding our own paths of discovering Welshness, for we start from different ways of seeing, and bring our own needs with us. Also, as in the Celtic vision quest, the goal is changed by the journey towards it. It is like the story of Culhwch and Olwen, where the hero only completes half the tasks originally set, but takes on a series of new challenges along the way. Culhwch says to the giant Ysbaddaden who imposes each impossible task:

'It is easy for me to get that, though thou think it is not easy.' And each time the giant answers:

'Though thou get that, there is that thou wilt not get.'

These mythical tales help me through the labyrinth that is my own quest for Welshness, when I get lost in the maze of pluralism that is Wales now, trying to pick my particular path through the lures of competing cultural identities.

My needs include finding a land of our mothers that celebrates women's values as well as the land of our fathers that celebrates our 'warring defenders so gallant and brave'. So Rhiannon is one significant role model. She is the one who rides her white horse like the whirlwind when Prince Pwyll orders his knights to bring her to him, but gladly comes to him when he himself courteously invites her. It is her bright wits that save the day when Pwyll nearly loses her to a rival suitor by playing the generous lord and offering Gnawl anything in the world he wants (and it turns out he wants Rhiannon). Nor does she ever lose her compassionate integrity when disaster strikes. When her maids falsely accuse her of killing her own child to save themselves from blame after the infant has been spirited away in the night, she says to them, 'Poor creatures . . . accuse me not falsely . . . And if it be fear that is upon you, by my confession to God I will protect you.' They clung to their story and Rhiannon was punished, but at least she had tried.

The tale of Branwen, by contrast, shows the unacceptable face of woman in man's mythology. Her family marry her off to the Irish King Matholwch who mistreats her. She trains a starling to carry the story of her woes back to Gwynedd, whereupon Bendigeidfran and his warriors set sail and lay waste the whole island of Ireland. Branwen is called one of the 'Three Chief Ancestresses', but is powerless to prevent the slaughter. All she can do is heave a great sigh that breaks her heart. She dies crying out, 'Alas, Son of God, that ever I was born; two good islands have been laid waste because of me.'

They say that women in medieval Wales had greater freedom than in neighbouring countries. The laws of Hywel Dda set out women's rights in marriage and in the break-up of marriage. When a woman separated from her husband one partner would divide all the possessions into two halves and the other would choose which half to take. If the woman found her husband with another woman she could claim six-score pence

122

the first time, a pound the second time, and the right to separate the third time. But it was not all equal opportunity for:

> If it happens that a woman says shameful words to her husband, such as wishing a blemish on his beard or dirt on his teeth, or calling him a cur, law judges the payment of a *camlwrw* to her husband for every one of them, for every woman's husband is her lord; or, if he prefers it, let him strike her three blows with a rod as long as a man's forearm and as thick as a long finger, in any place except the head . . .

Now we have Equal Opportunities legislation putting pressure on the parts that Hywel Dda failed to reach, but a recent report from the Equal Opportunities Commission in Cardiff focuses on the absence of women from public life, on councils, on quangos and in local government, compared with other European Community countries. Why is this, I have to ask, since for me discovering Welshness includes sharing women's past and working in the present to help enrich women's opportunities in Wales. It has been heartening to be on the first 'master's' course in Women's Studies in Cardiff University, and to teach an evening class on Women, Spirituality and Religion in Aberystwyth's Extra-mural Department, because I need to find and help build networks here for the things that matter in any country. There are communities of interest and communities of shared causes as well as the traditional communities of place and language and culture.

Communities of interest, however, have to be grounded in their local and national cultures, so an incomer needs a whole new map of the imagination to be able to join in. I am still feeling my way here, but I try to fill in the blanks on the map by exploring the key figures and key ideas, past and present. There is the model of Welsh womanhood set out in the first journal for women, *Y Gymraes* (1851): 'faithful girls, virtuous women, thrifty wives and intelligent mothers who would instil Christian morality and virtue into the men and boys of Wales'. But going beyond that rather patriarchal view of women's potential are all the women who have managed to combine their valued home lives with speaking out in the wider world. There was Ann Griffiths the Montgomeryshire visionary who became an inspired hymn writer on a par with Williams Pantycelyn (though her hymns were only preserved by the good fortune of her maid having an excellent memory, while Pantycelyn's ran to several editions in his own lifetime). There was Ceridwen Brown of Aberdare who led the women of the South in the 1930s marches against unemployment and low-wage family poverty. There were the Women's Support Groups in the 1984 miners' strike, which helped many working-class women realise in their own everday lives that 'If you're committed you can't wait for anybody else, you must join in and get involved . . . We've got to do something for our future'. There is Red Flannel Films in Pontypridd making visible the hidden lives of women in Wales, and the women's publishers Honno, and the Women in Technology training and support group in Glamorgan. And embedded in the more traditional culture is the nationwide network of *Merched y Wawr* and Women's Institutes (and in my own valley the Cwmrheidol Ladies Guild), which gave warm support to women's home-based activities, but are gradually also turning outwards to face their communities' problems. *Merched y Wawr* in mid-Wales, for instance, has supported incomers learning the language by invitations to meetings and by arranging holiday stays with Welsh-speaking families.

Mabon the archetypal prisoner

One of the paradoxical figures in the Welsh and Irish hero tales is Mabon, who has to be rescued from his underground and under-river dungeon in Gloucester, to play his essential part in the vision quest. King Arthur's knights arrive on the back of their wise old salmon to save him, but still Mabon struggles against his own release. Modern psychological interpretations of this tale say that real freedom (of the self or of the nation) is more scary than clinging to the comfortable half truths that imprison us. The endless quest for self or national identity can only succeed when we escape from 'our side's' version of the truth, and build bridges to the other sides. The truth is poised in the middle of the see-saw. You have to be a nationalist to be an internationalist, as James Connolly observed. And to be a fully human nationalist you have to be an internationalist as well.

For me discovering Welshness includes seeking out the bridge-builders who are working to find the common ground rather than emphasise the divisions between all the polarities that exist in Welsh society. The litany of polarities is endless. There are nationalists and internationalists, Welsh speakers and non-Welsh speakers, English-speaking incomers and Welsh-learner incomers, chapel and church and goddess worshippers, fey and technocrat, *gwerin* and intelligentsia, bourgeois and hippies, feminists and patriarchs, farming communities and urban-industrial communities . . . Pouring across Offa's Dyke are not only 'white settlers' but 'green' smallholders seeking a way of life more *gwerinol* than the *gwerin*. As well as layabout hippies hoping for highs on magic mushrooms there are whole-earth hippies whose benders resemble the medieval Welsh huts described in Giraldus Cambrensis, or the squatters' turfed cabins of the seventeenth and eighteenth centuries, the *tai unnos* raised in a night on common land, often round, windowless, the smoke drifting out of a crude chimney in the conical roof.

Are there bridge-builders between all these potentially antagonistic elements? Who is working to release us from being prisoners of our particular half-truths? I have discovered *Pont*, which brings together incomers and local people through a network of activities all over the country. There is *Cymdeithas y Cymod* in the churches acting as a fellowship of reconciliation. *CYD* helps language learners meet native speakers and cross the bridge between cultures. The informal system, as always, is more important than the institutional system, so a lot depends on the minority of individuals who give their time and imagination in their own local communities to drawing newcomers into a better understanding of Welshness (and *vice versa*) through help with learning the language, or by sharing their social life and interests with incomers who want to discover the hidden Wales, but have not the nerve to turn up alone at the eisteddfod or the *noson lawen*, the local history lecture or the *Duchess of Malfi* performed in Welsh.

Positive Welshness and negative Welshness

When poised on the threshold of a different culture, another country, I begin to get glimpses of a different network of song-lines laid across the land, telling other stories than the ones I have heard about Wales in England, in Ireland and in Cardiff. I am reminded of the two (at least) versions of eighteenth-century Ireland that never communicated, as seen by Lecky through the Ascendancy mind, and the 'hidden Ireland' as seen by Daniel Corkery through the Gaelic literature of the Munster poets. In modern Ireland both still have their adherents, and in Wales I find myself confused by similar conflicting ways of seeing Welsh identity.

At regular intervals in the *Western Mail* and in *Wales on Sunday* there are letters from Joneses and Davieses or Morgans advocating getting rid of the language to prepare us for unity with Europe. Meanwhile the European Parliament is actively giving support to the languages and cultures of regional and ethnic minorities. As an Irish Member of the European Parliament said during the debate on the Kuijpers Resolution in support of this policy:

> Let us be absolutely clear. Linguistic and cultural diversity never causes conflict. It is the refusal of some people to accept diversity that causes problems and strife.

Living with two languages is a fact of life in Wales, to which both incomers and the indigenous population can respond either positively or negatively. A positive response in some parts can only be made by learning the language or by having one's children learn the language to help the survival of Welsh-speaking community schools. In other parts of the country the priority is simply for non-Welsh speakers, indigenous or incomer, to acknowledge and support the linguistic rights of the twenty per cent who speak the language. In the extreme cultural antagonisms of Ulster efforts to persuade people that cultural diversity is a richness and not a threat have included a series of programmes on the Irish language (in English) from BBC Northern Ireland (which used to worry about not offending the Orange Order). The southern Irish government too has published a very informative glossy booklet in English to explain the history and use of Irish. In Wales, I think the nearest thing to these is the visitors' guides to the National Eisteddfod. But then S4C and the Eisteddfod itself are seen as culturally exclusive and threatening by many English-speaking Welsh. Paradoxically too, a Welsh Labour Member of Parliament who attacked Dyfed's bilingual education policy as 'force-feeding inmigrant children' provoked a response both from Plaid Cymru and English-incomer parents, pointing out that access to two languages and two cultures is enriching beyond the immediate benefit of integrating with the local community.

The language is ever present in debates on national and cultural identity in Wales, hovering ghost-like even when unspoken. Managing bilingualism is a formidable task of keeping the formal and the informal systems in balance. It is a fine thing to have the language in the National Curriculum for every child to the age of sixteen, but to fanatical English speakers in Gwent it may look like the 'English not' imposed by nationalists, unless a way is found to give Welsh a wordly, more élite image. This may happen as a result of more teaching and media jobs for young Welsh speakers, or as a spin-off from the growing fashion for 'lesser-used languages' in the European Community. All over Europe there is a surge of adults learning minority languages, seeking 'small is beautiful'. There are places where Welsh-language Welshness has still a natural primacy. In Tŷ Mawr Wybrnant, birthplace of Bishop Morgan the first translator of the Bible into Welsh, the language is part of past and present. History is presented through landscape and buildings, words and people, from an inside view. The hidden Wales becomes a bit more visible. At the National Eisteddfod in Llanrwst in 1989 I had again a sense of overwhelming immersion in an everyday lived culture. But then I went to the exhibitions of painting and photography and felt a sense of unease at so much overt drawing on the past for images (of ruined cottages and mythical figures looming from desolate misty landscapes), rather than transmuting the past into a seedbed for reflection on the complex and diverse Wales in which we live. As Seumas Heany noted in his inaugural lecture in 1989 as Oxford's Professor of Poetry, the artist's job in a culture is to give us 'a counter-reality', to work against the grain of received ideas and vocabularies. As indeed Tony Conran has done in drawing on the *Mabinogi* for his recent play *Branwen*. He does not use the myth in any sentimental or nostalgic way, but injects into the original plot very current concerns of chauvinist hubris where the powerful speak to the powerful and shut out weaker voices.

Where do I go from here? My quest to discover Welshness carries on, and I am aware of being changed in the process. I bring my origins and life concerns to my new Welsh context, and the new Celtic connection gives me, curiously, more cultural breathing space than I used to feel in Ireland, where conflicting cultures are too close to the bone and the blood. There are comforting parallels for an escapee—the uses of satire, the warmth of individuals, the clash of tradition and modernities, the cultural identity crises. Wales, fortunately, also lacks Ireland's violent forms of nationalism, and that is important to me as a pacifist brought up in Ulster.

The challenge of becoming bilingual in some modest sense looms large at the moment. Though English will always be my natural tongue I have a strong feeling that it is an ethical courtesy to be able to speak Welsh in situations where otherwise people would have to change to English; that to read the language is to be better able to share Welsh ways of seeing the world; and that there are things I believe in (in the fields of religion and spirituality and feminism) which need to find a public in Welsh as well as in English. Underlying all that is the ghost of a conviction that the true test of any democracy is how it gives a voice to minorities of language, religion or culture that are in danger of being swamped by dominant cultures.

A CHRISTIAN CIVILISATION
Daniel Mullins

One of the small and very real pleasures of life is to dip into the works of the great medieval Welsh poets. I do not refer to reading them in the serious and disciplined way which would become a scholar. I mean rather that casual reading which is the privilege of anyone reasonably versed in the Welsh language. It brings you into contact with another age and another outlook from our own. It also reveals another way of comprehending God's world which is the characteristic of an indigenous and fully developed culture and civilisation. And I say 'God's world' because the Christian understanding of those two words is a powerful formative element in that civilisation which is the special creation of the historic people who are known as the Welsh—the foreigners in their own land.

The Welsh language is a quite extraordinary phenomenon. It is listed among the minor languages of Europe. It never was the spoken language of a very large group of people. Ever since it developed in this corner of the world from the older and more complex language of the pre-Roman inhabitants of these parts, its speakers could be numbered in thousands rather than in millions. And yet it produced a major literature. Because of its history and its special links with the inheritance of Rome, it also recorded that literature in manuscripts and made it the subject of study and of learned employment. The chronicler and the poet belonged to an honoured and respected profession. The language was the medium and the mould for the whole pattern of ordered living which this people developed for itself.

That Welsh will survive into the next millenium is an historic anomaly. The last independent Welsh prince died in 1282. To consolidate the conquest of Wales, Edward I established a chain of castles which would dominate the local communities. Towns were established, often around the castles, and inhabitants brought in from England as part of the process of controlling the life of the indigenous people. English law alone was administered in those towns and boroughs. Towns in Wales, with two notable exceptions, have always remained English-speaking and centres of another culture and way of life. The Tudor Act of Union abolished the Welsh language and any remaining vestiges of native law as far as public life and administration were concerned. England was now the official name of the area of both countries. In the last century, a system of compulsory education was

128

introduced. For the framers of the system and the legislation, the Welsh language was a badge of the backwardness and even immorality of the people which education would remove forever. When the leaders of the Welsh people promoted and established a University for Wales, there was no place within it for the historic language of this people. By the laws of probability and of men, the language should have disappeared long ago. To explain the survival of the language one looks again at its literature. For a developed and cultivated literature enshrines the memory of a people. It expresses the culture by which the spiritual values of a people were developed and preserved. It outlines, too, the civilisation by which they ordered their communal lives and gave continuity to their social arrangements.

I want briefly to try to outline some of the characteristics of Welsh civilisation as they are revealed to anyone who bothers to master the language. In Welsh literature we see an ordered world which looks to its past in order to guide its present. Part of the responsibility of the poet was to preserve the memory of his people. That memory reached back to their origins as a people. The Welsh saw themselves as collateral relatives of the Romans and claimed links with Troy and the origins of Europe. The poet, too, chronicled and preserved the origins of families and genealogies. These things were not just fabricated conceits; they spelled out the links within the society and the responsibilities which those links imposed.

An important part of the Welsh literary tradition is the corpus of Law books, the handbooks of legal practitioners. These set out in precise detail the whole set of relationships, duties, rights and responsibilities which knit together the life of the people. Authority is the prerogative of those who accept the duty of defending the life and property of their subjects and who will ensure that rights are upheld and, if need be, enforced.

At the heart of society as conceived in Welsh literature and law, is the family. It extends across the age-groups and the generations. It carries with it family rights which apply equally to men and women and to those born in or out of wedlock. It imposes a responsibility for the behaviour of individual members and consequences to be borne by all for the misdeeds as well as the achievements of members. It was this far-reaching family concept which made Welsh society incapable of competing with the more restrictive and therefore more concentrated concept which the feudal barons brought from Normandy. Human nature is acquisitive and selfish. In trying to counteract these faults, Welsh society could not defend itself effectively against those who recognised

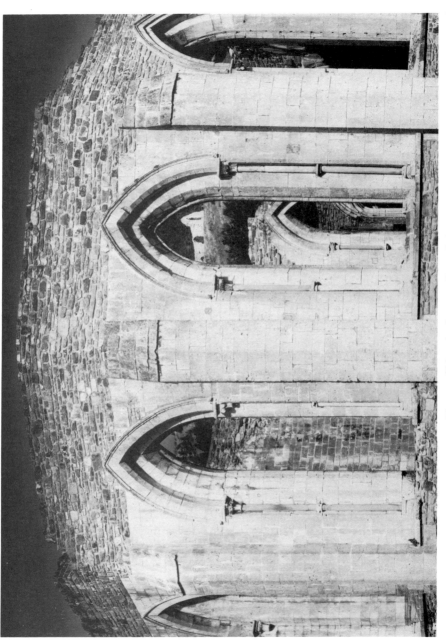

Margam Abbey, by Suzanne Greenslade

no such limitations. In another age when the true cost and the havoc caused by an unrestrained acquisitive society are becoming obvious, we have at hand another vision of social values and relationships which is at once more humane and more gentle.

The links that bind society are not only those of blood and family relationships. They include a shared understanding of the meaning and purpose of life and an accepted awareness of the common background and history that has made the speakers of this language a unique people. Historical awareness in this sense is always a combination of legend, traditions and a folk memory of events which have shaped the development of a people. When that people develops civilisation, all of that becomes part of the weave of its literature and its recorded annals and of its own sense of identity. A people's sense of identity always assumes a common past and shared concern in and responsibility for its future.

Urban and imperial civilisations have left monuments in architecture and sculpture. Neither the political nor the social organisation of Welsh life followed these directions. The monument by which it enriched the world is the great corpus of its literature. And literature was not the private concern of the few. Rather does it enshrine the whole fabric of ordered life—in its legal structure, its chronicling of events and its public celebration of its ideals, its hopes and its entertainment.

Classical Welsh poetry is formal and follows precise and intricate rules and patterns. To achieve the mastery of language which it required, needed long schooling and much practice. The enjoyment of that mastery was not confined to the few. Even a fairly cursory acquaintance with the poems of Dafydd ap Gwilym reveals at least three levels of composition and so of intended audience. There is the very formal and deliberately archaic use of language which carried its message for the importance of the subject of the poem. Then there is the nature and love poetry which follows many conventions which were shared by a medieval audience and which are often quite lost on the modern reader. It is very difficult for us to come to terms with the more relaxed attitudes and mores of an age which never knew either Jansenism or Puritanism in its formal religious and moral teaching. Then there is what in modern terminology one would call the pub poetry, though that probably gives a very misleading picture of what a tavern in the middle ages was like. This poetry was written as part of the social entertainment which was intended for everybody. Many of Guto Glyn's poems were intended to entertain the Welsh soldiery relaxing from the battlegrounds of France. And by that time not all the recruits to an army were the sons of

131

knights and squires and landed gentry. The religious poetry linked with Siôn Cent was certainly not intended for one section of society.

There are few civilisations of which it can be said that their law books are high literature. In Wales these books represent the fusion into a new entity of the age-old inheritance of Celtic peoples and the *Ius Gentium* which was part of the Roman legacy. And the highly-developed language of Wales was the instrument for this development. The sharp precision of thought and the fine honing of accurate terminology and expression combined to produce a corpus of work that illustrates the organising ability, the breadth of social vision and the humorous toleration of human foibles which is one of the great monuments of Christian Europe.

A characteristic of Welsh people today, a love of words and a willingness to be swayed by oratory has very deep roots. This land of Wales has produced few great indigenous buildings. The castles and even the cathedrals are mainly the work of conquerors. Other forms of visual and performing arts did not have the necessary conditions for development and wide use. But a love of language and an appreciation of the cultivation of forms of artistic expression was, and remains, central to the fabric of social communication and cultural relaxation. It cannot be appreciated or understood, even when transferred to another language, without a working knowledge of Welsh. Modern Wales, in all its variety, is incomprehensible to those who neglect the past from which it came.

IMAGES OF WALES
Fiona Bowie

Revolting students (the pun intentional), Welsh extremists, long hair, pop music and the drugged-up flower people; images of the 1960s and early 1970s, of all that was disapproved of. Too young or compliant to capture the spirit of change, I agreed with my elders that they all represented degeneration: them, not us. The only family history of Wales was the story of descent, on my maternal grandmother's side, from Judge Jeffries, 'the Hanging Judge', who various members of the family were said at times, when tempers were frayed, to resemble. Although I could feel passionately about the Highland clearances and treachery of the Campbells at Glencoe, the blacking-out of English roadsigns in Wales appeared the height of pettiness. And anyway, Wales was so far away. The four-hundred miles to Edinburgh was only a fraction of the distance from the south of England to . . . To where? I doubt whether fifteen years ago I could have named a single Welsh town, or at least have placed it correctly on the map. Cricieth was where strange things come out of the sea, and the name 'Abergavenny' sounded vaguely romantic (like 'Dar-es-Salaam'). If there was any part of Wales that might be worth getting to know it was surely the intriguing sounding 'little England beyond Wales', that mysterious yet comfortingly familiar place way out to the west.

As a postgraduate student in Oxford I used to supplement my grant by working in the college lodge (reception). At the beginning of my second year there a student, ostensibly buying stamps, picked out a name in the college list and asked me how I would pronounce it. I didn't know him well enough to realise that it was his own name, and was too slow to perceive that this was a crucial test. I am glad to say I passed, and within a few weeks I was on the train to Cardiff to meet my future in-laws. Prepared to put aside my twenty-three years of ignorance and prejudice, and to discover the rural idyll of Wales that my mentor in Welshness assured me was just over the border, I watched eagerly for my first glimpses of the promised country. Cwmbrân, Newport and the docks, the derelict areas that back onto railway sidings, neatly ordered suburbia, bilingual signs—toilets/*toiledau*, park/*parc*, Cardiff/*Caerdydd*. I must confess that I was disappointed. The countryside could hardly compare with Scotland, as I had been led to expect, and Cardiff failed to match the grandure and excitement of Edinburgh. The signs seemed merely ridiculous. I'm sure my lack of enthusiasm must have been a let down, but there was no getting away from the fact that Wales and Cardiff had lived up to my earlier prejudices, rather than to my recently acquired expectations.

I was ready to believe that there was more to Wales than my first impressions had revealed and we spent a week one summer in a friend's holiday cottage in Pembrokeshire. We watched the locals frequenting the public house by the back door long after closing time, enjoyed the fresh creamy milk from the farm, and profusion of wild flowers in the hedgerows. I saw how my husband both savoured talking Welsh to the farmers in the local, and was embarrassed that I was so obviously English. St. David's I loved, like Llantwit Major it was a town that looked 'English', that is, it was attractive, a relief to the eyes after the drabness of most of the Welsh towns and villages we had seen. How could people live in such lovely countryside and build such ugly houses? It was several

133

years before I learned to appreciate the solidity and more reserved character of Welsh market towns and to accord the little hamlets which dot the countryside the status of villages.

Another holiday, this time walking through mid and north Wales. The beauty, both gentle and rugged, of the scenery, enchanted me. My Welsh by this time consisted of a sentence about the dog peeing and *odi* or *odw*, which I threw in whenever I was required as a conversation partner in Welsh. I began to glimpse both the fun of speaking Welsh as a private language and the sense of acceptance into a small Welsh-speaking world that could follow. Moving to north Wales and enrolling in a Welsh course were simultaneous and both seemed perfectly natural. I could not envisage remaining monolingual English in a Welsh community, anymore than I could live in Germany, as we had for two years, without learning German.

To remain monolingual in Bethesda is to be forever an outsider. This perception was brought home to me during a concert in aid of Plaid Cymru in the recently opened Neuadd Ogwen. The sense of community was pulsating, but what was that community? Not a cross-section of the population but those who had treasured and preserved the language. Local people congratulating themselves and one another on something alive and precious, conscious that they were one of the last bastions of 'Welshness', an island in the midst of a sea of anglicisation. Ordinary people, our neighbours, as well as local dignitaries and the Welsh intelligentsia. The literary society lectures, the *Talwrn y Beirdd* competitions, eisteddfodau, *nosweithiau llawen*, all celebrations of community, a community which is still solidly Welsh-speaking, and into which those who take the plunge to learn Welsh are warmly welcomed.

Back in Oxford for a seminar I was introduced to a Welshman, and we exchanged a few words in that language. The warm, informal style of communication which I have come to associate with Wales contrasted starkly with the quick, sharp and competitive atmosphere, congenial in its own way, of Oxford academic life. 'Where do I live? Where is my husband from? His father, mother, grandfather, grandmother . . .?' I grew up in a village where I knew and was known. This knowing, belonging and placing of people, their family history and ups and downs is paradoxically one of the homecomings in Wales. From my own village experience I am well aware that two or three generations go into the making of a 'local'. In a way, Welsh-speaking Wales is a village, inter-locking networks of relatives and neighbours. As one of an itinerant tribe I do not belong or expect to belong in that way. Nevertheless, without sharing in a past which is rooted in Wales, I can enjoy the stability which belonging to a small community engenders.

The sense of straddling two contrasting worlds was heightened by a dinner party. On my right was an English speaker. The conversation, intelligent and cultivated, could be repeated in Surrey, Oxford, or in any English middle-class home or university town. To my left was a Welshman, and a whole world of Welsh sentiment, a cultural storehouse which, to the curious foreigner who possesses the key, is full of wonders. Here was a history, a mythology, a sensibility, a poetry, a literature and a host of unknown names, an understanding of politics and an experience of religion which was all new to me. This Wales is as foreign to me as Germany, in many ways more so, but it is precisely this combination of otherness, together with a sense of belonging, which is *my* Wales. With the respect and awe with which we must always approach 'other people's dreams' it is all there waiting to be discovered.

An anthropologist steps out of his or her own culture in order to see what is familiar from a new perspective. In Wales I have come to appreciate England and my debt to it. I never thought of myself as English, and still don't, but England is the country in which I grew up and was educated and it has played its part in shaping the person I have become. But I have learnt much from Wales, perhaps lessons I could have learnt elsewhere, but it so happens that it is Wales which has been my tutor. I have learnt what it is to live under the shadow of a more powerful, often arrogant and blind, language and culture. I have learnt what it means to have your life dominated by economic forces over which you have no control. I have learnt what it is to salvage self-respect from centuries of prejudice, from the voices which tell you that what is most intimate, the language you speak, is somehow deficient. Every culture has its tale to tell and the message is invariably the same. That there is more than one way to doing and of being, that what is right for you is not necessarily right for me, and that one and one make three and not two. It is not Wales or England, incomer and local, Welsh-speaking Wales or English-speaking Wales, but both and all. Each person and every culture, is unique and precious. We need to bring our own particular gifts and to learn to enjoy and share those of others. What emerges is then a new reality which both respects differences and celebrates what is best in each of us.

ADNABOD, HANFOD, CYMREICTOD
M.A.K. Duggan

A nation . . . is a phenomenological construct . . . in which individuals communicate . . . the charged space of territory and the charged story of their past.

Ninian Smart

> Beth yw adnabod? Cael un gwraidd
> Dan y canghennau . . .
> Beth yw bod yn genedl? Dawn
> Yn nwfn y galon.
> Beth yw gwladgarwch? Cadw tŷ
> Mewn cwmwl tystion.

Waldo Williams

> (What is *adnabod*? Finding one root
> Under the branches . . .
> What is it to be a nation? A special gift
> In the heart's deep places.
> What is patriotism? Keeping house
> In a cloud of witness.)

It is notoriously difficult to define the concept of nationality in any sense other than the political or legal. The latter criteria are established today by reference to the trappings of the nation-state which gave rise to them, yet it should be remembered that this is a modern European creation, whose imposition on, or imitation by, other races has frequently been incongruous or even disastrous, and which would, moreover, have been incomprehensible in Europe itself a few centuries ago. There remain perennial problems for the tidy-minded: the Kurds, perhaps, or the Armenians; while the complexities of African tribalism and the rhetoric of pan-Arabism are constant reminders that the world cannot successfully be disposed according to the principles of the Peace of Westphalia or the Congress of Vienna.

In the small area designated 'Wales' on maps, legal and political considerations of nationhood were relevant only to the sale of alcohol until recently. He or she who seeks to ground a personal consciousness of being Welsh in empirical reality has to make do with outward and visible signs less reassuringly solid than armorially-embossed folders that request and require, the boast of heraldry and the pomp of long-departed power—a few cryptically-inscribed stone crosses in the back of some country church, perhaps, or a mosaic already broken by the tractors passing down the streets of the little market town where it was laid a short time ago. The chances of history threw up many political anomalies in Europe—Monaco, Andorra, and the rest of those charming curiosities whose economies survive on stamp-collecting and tax-avoidance—but other entities lost out, and Wales was among them.

Yet *Cymreictod*, Welshness, has objective existence in the Popperian sense, for it has had observable effects on the development of Britain and on individual lives, and it has been open to manipulation for desired ends. Consider some examples at random: Freud's opinion that Welshness was an ineradicable part of the psyche of his disciple, Ernest Jones; the manner in which a Welsh or 'Ancient British' mythology was manufactured and, contrary to any logic, attached to England for the service of Empire during the last century; the rise of religious noncon-formity in eighteenth- and nineteenth-century Wales compared with the progress of the movement in England. It cannot be denied that the consciousness of being Welsh has been interpreted as something quite definite and significant, by both those who possess it and those who perceive it from the outside.

This does not render any easier the task of defining Welshness, or of establishing criteria by which a Welshman might vindicate his right to the title (if such were thought to be necessary). With regard to the parallel notion of English identity the example of Eliot is salutary, for inasmuch as Raymond Williams exposed the numerous flaws and weaknesses of his writings on the national culture, without detracting from the greatness of the man or the merits of his attempt, so have others done unto Williams and his conceptions of class-loyalty and popular art.

Of course, the task of defining Welshness becomes a great deal more straightforward than was Eliot's by the use of one criterion. What, it might be asked, sustained a national consciousness in the mind of the Welshman after the death of his last native prince, after the defeat of Glyndŵr in the final attempt to establish the institutions of an inde-pendent Wales, after the Act of Henry VIII which effectively assimilated Wales into England? *Cymraeg*, the Welsh language, obviously: *Cymraeg*, and the particular culture of which it was the progenitor. The only mystery would seem to be the remarkable resilience of this culture in the face of pressures which virtually obliterated its Celtic cousins, Cornish and Manx, and rendered the Gaelic tongues of Ireland and Scotland relatively unimportant as nationally cohesive forces. Quite apart from any other virtues, this hypothesis has the simplicity to be readily grasped: what makes the Welshman Welsh is his use of an ancient language, which will, of course, influence his thought and his life, and thus the society he creates, by that mutual interaction which most of us can accept and few of us claim to understand in detail.

That this assertion was substantially true up to the beginning of this century, and valid to a large extent for many years afterwards, cannot be denied. For whatever mysterious reasons, Welsh emerged from its parent British speech, almost a millennium-and-a-half ago, as a literary language of considerable sophistication, and the peculiar position of the skilled artist-in-words in Welsh society was a prominent feature until very recently, and remains recognisable today. Matthew Arnold was one of the first to examine this relationship between Welsh literature and Welsh thought and, if many of his presuppositions and conclusions are unacceptable to modern scholarship and sensibility, his seminal insights were nevertheless remarkable in their context and are still valuable to the student of Wales and its people. Similarly, the all-important place of religion, and particularly of Dissent, in post-Reformation Welsh life may be understood—in part—by a realisation that the only book that the majority of Welshmen ever read in their own tongue until the last century was *Y Beibl,* and that they read it without the guidance of any ecclesiastical tradition because of the eclipse and partial anglicisation of the Established Church of the time. As is widely known, Bishop Morgan's Bible, his own revision of his original translation, was the effective saviour of literary Welsh, a language of oral transmission; *Cymraeg y Beibl* is still the equivalent of the expression 'the Queen's English'.

Both the literary and the religious traditions of Wales, as mediated through its language, were employed in the deliberate manipulation of Welshness referred to earlier. On the one hand, there is the use made of Welsh legend and Welsh poetry by that flawed genius, Iolo Morganwg, and his circle; Iolo turned them to the service of egalitarianism and emergent democracy in the fashion that the historian Gwyn Alf Williams so admires, and attempted to fuse Biblical religion with a spurious 'Druidism' and arrive at continental Deism as the result. On the other hand, the same corpus of literature, suitably translated, was the basis of the successful manufacture of a Victorian 'King Arthur and his Knights', types and models for the English Gentlemen, the Man the Empire Wants, while the apparent independence of the Celtic Church was invoked to vindicate the position of the Church of England and cry down the pretensions of Rome.

So far, so good; and yet the hypothesis I have been discussing, an unqualified assertion of the central role of the language in supporting the Welsh identity, will no longer do. For the majority of Welsh people—that is, people who believe themselves to be Welsh, express their claim to being Welsh strongly, and with some pride, are offended when it is suggested that they are anything other than Welsh—are unable to speak more than a few words of the Welsh language. It is on behalf of these people, to whom the 'Taliesin tradition', to use Emyr Humphreys' term, would not appear to be very relevant, and to whom *capel*, the Welsh chapel, is a dimly-remembered childhood relic, or simply a word engraved over the door of the local bingo-hall, that Gwyn Alf Williams and his colleague, Dai Smith, have spoken. They set out conceptions of Welshness that seem more appropriate to the present time and to the environment of south-east Wales.

If Emyr Humphreys and Ned Thomas have presented the Taliesin tradition (of Welsh-speaking Wales) eloquently and critically to those unfamiliar with it, Gwyn Alf Williams and Dai Smith have argued equally forcefully for the acceptance of the Welshness of the industrial Valleys, Blaenau Gwent and Blaenau Morgannwg. Saunders Lewis wrote, as is well-known, a poem describing the dereliction of Dowlais some fifty years ago, and included the crucial line, '*Yma bu unwaith Gymru* . . .'—'Here once was Wales . . .' The poem in its entirety is complex, and is not, in any event, representative of all that he had to say about his nation and its people. Yet, as they stand, the words invite an immediate and angry response, for the inhabitants of Dowlais were, and to our shame still are, among the most materially deprived in Wales (and in Britain), and very few of them could be held responsible for the destruction of their environment or the disappearance of the culture that sustained their fathers. As R. S. Thomas said, a farmer has little time for art when he is docking mangels, and is not to be blamed for it. The people of Dowlais, and of Penrhiwceiber and Blaenclydach and Glyncorrwg, were not docking mangels but cutting coal and smelting iron, and doing very little but attending to the necessities of survival apart from that. The bonds of community that grew up between them under the shared weight of suffering, the remarkable respect that they entertained for learning and the time that they somehow managed to devote to its pursuit, their perennial hope in humanity, and the dry humour with which all these things were spiced—these have been documented, in fact and in fiction, too conspicuously to require detailed account. They exist today, precariously, in the very different climate of the era; the real tragedy of the Valleys is that so much has conspired to promote somewhat different priorities in an altogether new dispensation.

It is unjust to stigmatise their inhabitants as half-breeds and turncoats, and still less as *bradwyr* (traitors), because they have lost, through no fault of their own, the language of their grandparents and all that went with it. Everything else about them proclaims, very loudly indeed, that they, too, are of the *Cymry*, and in the tale of the sorrows of Wales their lament is as great as any.

Glamorgan is the *bro* where I came to my own consciousness of Wales as more than a name to be inserted, optionally, at the end of my address; but reflection upon it, and upon the circumstances that left me monoglot English, like most of my contemporaries, enhances the complexity of the problem of Welsh identity. My childhood was divided between the north-east, not far from Rhondda, where I was born, and a village in the west of the county, in Cwm Tawe; my teens were spent in Bro Morgannwg, the rural Vale of Glamorgan in the south-east. In Cwm Tawe, Welsh was spoken around me constantly, and in Rhondda it was latent in the background of speech, emerging occasionally on the lips of my neighbours, but in the Vale it was scarcely more than a memory. My parents understood little of it, and spoke none, while the grandparents with whom I spent much of my time were the one half-Pembroke-half-English and the other all Pembroke; moreover, the Pembroke in question was Pembroke south of the Landsker (another of those linguistic boundaries that has to be accommodated in any understanding of Wales and its people), and they, too, had no Welsh whatsoever. As for the other side of my family, it was firmly Cardiff-based, and composed of borderland-Welsh elements with a dash of the Irish that gives me, like many other Welshmen, a name well outside the common range by which origins in the Principality are recognised. Within the bounds of my family and the environment of my formative years—the Valleys, the Vale, Cwm Tawe and Cardiff—there were four very different speeches and ways of life, discounting my grandfather's Pembroke dialect, and the only thing that they had in common, perhaps, was that representatives of each of them would, if asked, have replied to the effect that they were not English.

Such a diversity within a comparatively small area rides roughshod over precise definitions and delineations, but there were still more anomalies in the Wales that presented itself to me. What, for example, was one to make of the 'Bracchi', the third- and fourth-generation Italians who are so much part of the Valleys yet maintain their language and Roman Catholicism, and constantly renew their ties with the Val' Ceno, *bro* of their fathers? No doubt they will be assimilated eventually; no doubt the names of Jo Forlini and Gino Moruzzi will pass forever

140

from pictures of the Aberaman 1st. XV and the Tyntyla Constitutional Club Committee. But for the present the paradox remains. The most moving and evocative pictures of Valleys life in the last half of this century are painted, almost obsessively in his exile, by a man who taught at an English public school; he comes from Blaengwynfi and his name is Carpanini.

The most important of these anomalies in my own life was my school. Cowbridge Grammar was at that time the only state-controlled boarding-school in Wales, although boarders were in the minority and, because of its history and because of the prevailing disapproval of selective secondary education, it is generally assumed to have been very much an English establishment in ethos; the biographies of two of its 'old boys', the poet Alun Lewis and the actor Anthony Hopkins, have each emphasised this in their explanations as to why neither was particularly in sympathy with it. Certainly it was very different from the other schools in Glamorgan. But whatever it was, it was not English. Few have stopped to examine the culture of the Vale of Glamorgan, of which it was for centuries a celebrated institution, for the Vale is similarly assumed to be essentially English. It did, indeed, become anglicised in the Middle Ages; but Welsh returned, on a scale unequalled elsewhere, during the last century, only to decline again in this. Despite its longstanding connections with the English West Country, due to seaborne trade, it retained its Celtic idiosyncrasies; those defunct trade-routes were the last remnant of a time when the Vale was the cradle of Welsh civilisation, sending its missionaries far across Europe and receiving the cultural heritage of the Ancient World and the wisdom of the Desert Fathers in return. The long vowels once characteristic of *Cymraeg y Fro* declare that Tythegstone and Flemingstone and Siginstone are not, after all, to be confused with Moreton-in-the-Marsh and Chew Magna. But genuine anglicisation is now progressing apace: the conversion of the Vale into a dormitory area for an amorphous motorway corridor the colour of Swindon; only in retrospect, perhaps, will it be realised how Welsh it was. Cowbridge Grammar School fitted into it comfortably, having worn itself a niche over a very long time. Any pretensions to public-school status it might have had fifty years earlier had disappeared; it would have been laughed out of court by the genuine English article. In common with most other schools in east Glamorgan at that time, it allotted a deplorably insignificant position on its curriculum to the teaching of Welsh; unique to it were its senses of community and of continuity in a learned tradition, and it was under the influence of a

141

number of my mentors there that my own sense of the place of these elements in Wales was first clarified.

Like most expatriates, I began to examine my consciousness of my country and my roots when I left it. Only a few hours away from Wales, I was nevertheless aware of being among a different people; I was quite content in London, but that did nothing to alter the fact that I was away from home. It was not a burning sense of exile, which would have been ludicrous in its context, or a sense of loneliness in the crowd, which I did not feel, that concentrated my mind. It was simply the effect of distance, of separation from one of the fixed points in my life, that led me to contemplate Wales in relation to myself and to others. It is extremely difficult to produce a watertight definition of nationality, and beyond my mediocre ability to do so. But were I to try, I would have to start with the idea of articulating one's own identity, to oneself and to the outside world, in the context of a community and in terms of that community. We have been told that there is no such thing as society, only individuals. Insofar as some abstract conception of society cannot take precedence over the individual's humanity, this is right, and the totalitarianism of the present century has surely taught us as much. No doubt there are other possible interpretations of the pronouncement, at best unpalatable and at worst wholly unsatisfactory, for she who made it was not Welsh, and knew nothing of *cymdeithas* or *cymuned*, and not much of *cytundeb* either.

Trying to characterise aspects of Welshness in the context of a community is still a dangerous business, because it is easy to descend to the 'Jones the Shop' level, and yet I cannot but remember that Glyn the Milk really did deliver my semi-skimmed until recently, and that the local schools-supply officer was genuinely known as Dai Chalk. These names were conferred, or appeared, self-consciously, in perpetuation of the joke, because we have a tendency to self-mockery. The humour was in the fact that such titles, natural enough in a small population sharing a limited range of surnames, are also part of that national joke, in which we mock our self-presentation to the world in general and the English in particular—or, it may be, mock their stupidity in taking us at face value when we have carefully manufactured the face.

Welshness must always be seen in relation to England, first and foremost, it seems to me, if only because England is the one nation with which Wales shares a border and, thanks to our history, the rest of the world has known little or nothing about us. A complex self-concealment, particularly from the Englishman, is characteristic of the Welshman. Sometimes, indeed, this self-concealment is most effective when he is apparently engaged in a strident proclamation of his own identity, if only because the unwary are encouraged to make assumptions of an understanding they don't possess and, plunging on, swiftly encounter a barrier through which they cannot pass. The problem is that on the other side of the barrier we, too, are not sure what is there, although we know that there is something.

A number of Welsh traits can, arguably, be traced to this fear of self-definition, an uncertainty as to who we are: Nonconformity in religion, for example, and radicalism in politics. There have been distinguished Welsh communists, it is true, but generally the Welshman has not had the surety of aim of the true revolutionary or the ruthlessness that goes with it—just the conviction that questions must be asked even if no definite answers are available, that the Establishment must be challenged and the *status quo* must be altered, that everything is not for the best in this far from best of all possible worlds. It is for this conviction, I believe, rather than for any Utopian vision, that Welshmen have died, from John Penry to Dic Penderyn.

Then there is our fierce attachment to place and our stubborn loyalty to friends. We each live in a particular *bro*, by which I mean both a landscape and a community—Blaenclydach, not merely Rhondda, and still less, Glamorgan. The landscape becomes integral to our existence, whether it is the great shoulder of Bannau Sir Gâr seen through the farm window or the shabby little terrace called Prosser Street of which the house is part. It is not a conscious appreciation in any aesthetic sense, just an appropriation of a view which becomes normative in our lives and which we carry with us, positively or negatively, as 'home'. If you are uncertain as to who you are, it is useful to know where you are; *Cymru* itself is merely your *bro* writ large, and its inhabitants are the larger *cymdeithas*, the *Cymry*, whose very name implies as much. Across the border is altogether vaguer: up England way.

Most of all, perhaps, there is a brooding on memory and a sense of loss, a retracing of *llwybrau gynt*, the certainty that, whatever the future may bring, it will not bring back. Someone once suggested to me that this was typical of all Celts, because it embodied a folk-memory of their eclipse as a great European power, a subconscious recollection of their decline into the tiny nations that they constitute today. While that may be true, if one accepts the idea of a collective unconscious in the first place, it is not the whole story. One cannot comprehend the cry of 'How long, O Lord?' on the lips of a Jew in terms of the diaspora and of Auschwitz alone; and one cannot comprehend the Welshman's *hiraeth* for the past solely in terms of the Gallic Wars or the destruction of Manaw

143

Gododdin. To many, and to many Welshmen, it has seemed a foolish and irrelevant tendency, and it can undoubtedly assume that negative force in individual lives, but it is frequently a strength, conferring an insight into human sorrow and a corresponding degree of compassion for our fellows. In any case, valuable or not, we cannot dispose of it that easily, try as we may.

Such then, is something of my understanding of *Cymreictod*, for which I do not claim any privileged position. It is merely part of one man's self-perception, and it is open to criticism on the grounds of imprecision and woolly thinking, on the one hand, and to ridicule for pretentiousness, on the other. Yet I would like to believe that it is not entirely without merit, or totally wide of the mark. A generalisation is always bound to fail to account for some aspect of the individual, by definition, and when one is attempting a discussion which approaches the mystery of human identity, then failure is guaranteed.

But one point remains to be made, as far as Welsh identity is concerned, and it brings me back to the language, to the exposition of Emyr Humphreys and the arguments of Saunders Lewis. I came to *Cymraeg*, as a non-Welsh speaker, by a variety of routes. I was interested in Welsh history in general and in certain aspects of local history in particular; I was an enthusiastic reader of Anglo-Welsh literature, or, lest that convenient term offend, of the literature of Welshmen who wrote in English; I had a large number of Welsh-speaking friends and colleagues. Last of all, I loved words for their own sake and, in those of R. S. Thomas, thought increasingly of Welsh, 'all those good words and me outside them'. Later, however, I began to see that there was another, overwhelming reason. What created Welshness, what still creates it, is the language. I believe that the cultures of those areas of Wales which are, for historical reasons, English-speaking, of the Valleys, of the Vale of Glamorgan, and of Cardiff, for instance, are of intrinsic value in themselves. But what went to their making, what prevents their being English cultures, and what sustains them if only by contrast, in tension with them, is *Cymraeg*.

> Ni sylwem arni. Hi oedd y goleuni, heb liw.
> Ni sylwem arni, yr awyr a ddaliai'r arogl
> I'n ffroenau. Dwfr ein genau, goleuni blas.
> Ni chlywem ei breichiau am ei bro ddi-berygl.
>
> (We did not notice her. She was the light, without colour.
> We did not notice her, the air which carried the scent
> To our nostrils. Our mouths' water, the light of taste.
> We did not feel her arms around her unendangered *bro*.)

Without *Cymraeg*, neither *Cymru* nor *Cymreictod* can survive, and arguments that the Welsh can go on making their own identity, manufacturing their own myth, without it, fail to convince me. The Cornish identity is a pitifully frail thing, clinging, as it has to, to an accent, a few place-names that nobody very much understands, and a parliament that no longer sits. Wales can easily tread the same path, as Saunders Lewis pointed out so magnificently; whether it will, despite the tremendous revival of interest in *Cymraeg* in Glamorgan and Gwent, and the genuine and fruitful efforts of many to acquire the language depends on policies made outside Wales.

While I have no intention of veering into a discussion of such policies, because I am not qualified to do so in the detail that it would require to produce a genuine critique, a few points are obvious. English is the most successful language in the world; Welsh cannot compete with it on equal terms, and could not were every Welshman fluent in his native tongue. Further, the attitudes which perceive rural England as nothing more than a potential building-site, extended adventure-playground or picturesque retirement-home will, when applied to Wales, extirpate the roots of the language by destroying those communities where it is constantly spoken in everyday life. The *laissez-faire* approach of most British administrations will thus lead to the extinction of Welsh no less surely, if more slowly, than the invocation of the doctrine of market forces and the 'freedom-of-choice' shibboleth of the present government.

Above all, what makes me pessimistic is my knowledge of a sad phenomenon: *anneall mawr y Saeson*, the great incomprehension of the Englishman, his incomprehension of why the Welshman should seek to assert his Welshness, why he is not content to be 'British', a term which he himself would not use in any other context, since he understands it to be synonymous with 'English'. At its worst, this attitude is manifested in the sort of irritable contempt that led to the demolition of Penyberth and the drowning of Welsh valleys earlier this century. At its best, it is a sort of patronising amusement or indulgence, an assumption of the superiority of English culture in some non-existent league table, a stereotyping assessment of Welshness as a matter of irrelevant and boring sensitivities, of a hopelessly unrealistic and cranky provincialism, of meaningless rhetoric and melodramatic rant, easily dispelled by a little hard-headed English common sense, of an altogether narrow and blinkered outlook on the world. I strongly suspect that, for a nation brought up to the mythological consciousness of ruling the waves and running that world in a reality which confines it to half a small island, the boot is on the other foot: Welsh culture is the only culture that Little

England can still override or pointedly ignore when it chooses, maintaining the delusion of power. This is the real meaning of 'English domination', a term that represents neither medieval bones for tribal gnawing nor the ludicrous cant of 'armed occupation' beloved of a puerile few. Political independence for Wales, were such a thing to become possible, would be pointless if the language were to die: an unnecessary multiplication of entities.

Canon Donald Allchin, an Englishman as far from the common attitude to Wales as it is possible to be, has taken the English Christian to task over his failure to be aware of Welshness, and particularly of Welsh spirituality. I have not mentioned spirituality very much, although, as it happens, it was something else that led me to the language, as it led Allchin. It is very easy to become nostalgic and sentimental about one's roots and in talking of religion in Wales, if one regards it positively, one can come close to collectively sanctifying the Welsh. For this reason, among others, I have avoided much discussion of another distinctive characteristic of the Welshman, his perspective on his faith or his lack of it, which is rather different from that of the Englishman. When the latter asks the question 'Why bother?' about Wales and Welshness, the answer very quickly boils down to the store one sets on spiritual values.

The philosopher of religion Ninian Smart has stated that 'national consciousness is a blend of awareness, sentiment and sacrament'. The implications for Wales of this truth were expressed in the writing of Waldo Williams, whom I quoted earlier, for he recognised them with wounding clarity. There is little to be gained by the pseudo-erudition of references to Berdyaev, who influenced him, and Marcel, who could have done, because his lines need no gloss. The heart of true nationalism is *adnabod*, for which, ironically, there is no precise word in English: deep personal knowledge, intimate understanding, recognition of another, of oneself in that other and the other in oneself. It underlies *cymundeb*, sustains *cymdeithas* and is alone the means whereby nation shall speak peace unto nation; but it transcends both nationalism and internationalism, for ultimately it is the true root of being, *gwreiddyn bod.*

Such a lofty conception of the nature of things may appear to be removed from a consideration of *Cymreictod* by several powers of magnitude. But this judgement itself displays a fundamental misunderstanding of *adnabod*. Profoundly convinced of the brotherhood of all men, Waldo saw it first in his own *bro*; *adnabod* was manifest in his family and in the trivia, if one wishes to use the word, of life in a remote

146

corner of a small country, conducted in the language of a dwindling minority.

I think it was the celebrated Rabbi Lionel Blue who recounted the anecdote of how, when a distinguished colleague was asked by an over-eager Anglican clergyman, 'What do the Jews think of Jesus Christ?', he replied, 'They don't'. Most Englishmen, if asked what they thought of Wales, would answer in similar vein. The point is that many Jews, including Rabbi Blue himself, have come to believe that they could profitably pay some attention to the best-known member of their race. Beyond any consideration of impending Eurocracy, of the continuation of a United Kingdom, of the demands of an enterprise society, of the merits of 'Small is Beautiful', even of whether one likes or dislikes male-voice choirs, one's attitude to the survival of Europe's oldest living literary language, and of the culture it has nurtured for almost two-thousand years, depends on whether one accepts the conception of value implicit in the image of the falling sparrow. *Cymro wyf fi*, I am a Welshman; and I do.

NOTES

hanfod—essence, intrinsic being; *bradwyr*—traitors; *Cymry*—the Welsh people, the term originally meaning something like 'comrades', with which its shared roots are obvious; *bro*—locality, region. It should be distinguished in this article from *Bro Morgannwg, Y Fro*, specific names for the area known in English as the 'Vale of Glamorgan'; *cymdeithas*—society; *cymuned*—community; *cytundeb*—agreement, concord; *llwybrau gynt*—literally, 'former paths', possibly 'The happy highways where I went/And cannot come again'; *hiraeth*—longing, especially for the past. There is an element in most of these terms which is basic to their usage in Welsh and defies translation, a specifically Welsh sense, as explained in relation to the word *adnabod*.

My view of *Cymreictod* was stimulated to crystallisation in conversations with Iolo Davies, George Askey, Jeff Alden, Norman Jenkins of Tal-y-fan, M. Glyn Thomas and the late Very Revd. J. F. Williams. I am also grateful to Simon North for his comments, as an Englishman, on the outcome. Ninian Smart's definition is taken from the paper 'Religion, Myth and Nationalism' in his collection *Concept and Empathy*. The poems of Waldo Williams quoted 'Pa beth yw dyn?' (What is Man?) and 'Yr Heniaith' (The Old Language), are part of the collection *Dail Pren*.

WHY DO I PUBLISH IN WELSH?
Judith Maro

Whenever I am asked why I publish my work in Welsh, I am lost for a quick answer. Is it too important for a mere witty riposte? Or doesn't it matter enough to give it deeper thought?

Of course it matters. There must be very good reasons indeed to choose, deliberately, to publish in a language that is not widely read. Moreover, it seems a ridiculous choice for one whose knowledge of Welsh is minimal and erratic. I don't only have to rely on a translator (and these, as is well known, are rather thin on the ground, difficult to find, and as often as not are unsatisfactory, as I've discovered to my cost —and I don't mean in financial terms alone!) The process takes a long time—it can be a matter of years. When finally the work is published, I am unable to read it with the close attention to detail required. I must rely on readers' reactions to tell me if my original meaning has got across. It does not always. Sometimes people complain about the inadequacy of the rendering which imputes a meaning to my words not intended by me. I am fortunate, however, in having found a first-rate translator in the Reverend William Williams of Machynlleth. But even there, younger readers complain that some of his idioms are too archaic and Scripture-ridden. Then there are difficulties in finding suitable publishers, who are mostly reluctant to undertake books which promise small financial return because of the potentially limited readership.

All in all, 'Why do I publish in Welsh?' is an awkward question, one of those family questions you can only answer when you get away from the family. I think I had to go to Ireland to attempt to answer it.

On St. Stephen's Green, next to the plush Shelbourne Hotel, there is a gap in the buildings. In terms of property development it must be the most expensive gap in Ireland. It is a Huguenot cemetery. There, adorned by the most sculpturesque wych-elm you ever saw, surrounded by the tall hotel and office blocks, the graves of centuries of Huguenots lie silent to the sky. Ireland is the jewel in the crown of Catholicism, yet here, on its most expensive plot, is a monument to their saintly opponents, the Huguenots. Ireland, like many a good wine, does not export well. Her image abroad of incessant violence belies this extraordinary tolerance—a very touching instance, that Huguenot cemetery —and I could think of many more. Strangely enough, it seems to me a monument of love, if you like, that tolerance so far removed from the violence of Ireland's reputation. And there is, despite all the violence

148

and the wars and killings the world over, a lot of love about. Why *do* I publish in Welsh?

Well, because I, a foreigner and a stranger, experienced a similar love and tolerance when I first came to Wales. As in Ireland, it was love born of local and definite identity. It was a *Welsh* welcome, none other. The Welsh aren't the only ones to accord it, but I happen to be writing about the Welsh, that people of a particular locale, with a particular language and a particular ethos. That identity was so strong that I knew I could never be *of* it, any more than the Huguenots could be of the Irish. But I knew, as they did, that however alien, I should be allowed to flourish in their midst and enjoy their affection, be accepted by them. That love was for real, as they say: it was made manifest in the first weeks, in wild, strange Cwm Pennant, when I cried for home and was comforted by a neighbour whose English was none too good but whose unfamiliar Welsh dishes, carried across the windswept pastures, were like manna.

So let the answer be simple: I publish in Welsh by way of returning that love. Having said that, however, I know there is more to it. First, as an Israeli, I soon cottoned on to something special about Wales. That acceptance of a stranger, that tolerance, was born of that locale I have mentioned, of belonging since time immemorial to a particular patch on God's earth. And that belonging I recognised at once. 'Oh Jerusalem, if I forget thee . . .' This belonging was inexorably wrapped up in an old tongue, which was integral to that identity. It could not exist without the Welsh tongue, its nuances and inherited memories. Just as you cannot be a definitive Israeli without speaking the Hebrew of the Bible, so the Welsh are definitive in their clinging to their ancient tongue against all pressures. I understand the pressures as well as the clinging. It is not just that the unit is small—'small is beautiful' can be rather glib—no, it is big, *very* big, in its way, concerned with things of the spirit, of people, of community.

All that was a long time ago. Since then my own children have grown up in Wales, attended Welsh schools in Welsh villages. My children are Welsh as I can never hope to be. More than that: they are deeply involved in the Welsh scene. They tell me that their conscious identity with Wales, her future, her culture and heritage as expressed in the Welsh language, is largely due to the upbringing my husband and I had given them. My husband, born and bred in Durham during the Depression, of a mining family dating back to south Wales, is an avowed Socialist yet fully sympathetic to Welsh aspirations. His convictions have left their mark on our children. My own background is different in kind if not in essence or ideology. The Land of the Bible is my home, my natural habitat. Perhaps that is why Wales appealed to me so readily, not only because of her Biblical tradition and place-names that echo home for an Israeli expatriate, but above all in her spirit of deeply ingrained culture based on centuries of love for the language, on her innate humanity, her tolerance and humour. All this is like a voice remembered from my childhood years, the years of our struggle for independence. I must have passed something of this on to my children. What is more right therefore than that I, in my turn, should try to 'repay' the debt of gratitude I owe Wales, my adopted country, and publish in the Welsh language, preserving the continuity, to add my literary output, such as it is, to the proud generations of Welsh writers. It is not presumption that dictates this but a sense of *rightness*.

Language is the vehicle of thought and inspiration, a precious instrument not to be treated lightly or neglected. Since my coming to Ireland I have come to realise that, far from dying, the Welsh language is alive and vibrant. The Irish government tried to foster the Gaelic by all the means at its disposal. It has largely failed. You hear no Gaelic spoken in most parts of Ireland, except in far corners of the west, among the poverty-stricken farmers of Connemara. The Irish, while enjoying political independence, are losing their distinctive mark that only divergence of tongues and cultures born of those tongues can provide. Welsh in comparison is very much alive. My own mother tongue, Hebrew, was revived through people using the language, teaching it at schools and universities, writing in it. While conditions were totally different and far more immediately compelling, I see a similarity of approach, of purpose. And so, against all odds, I publish in Welsh, because I have grown to love Wales and because I would hate to see the old language disappear in the uniformity of the mass-media age.

WELSHNESS
George Askey

A clear idea of personal identity can sometimes arise in an environment of cultural diversity. In my case, Welshness has never been an element which I have questioned. It appears complicated enough to have been born in the community of Rhymney, placed at the upper end of the Rhymney valley, of a Welsh-born mother who was bilingual in Welsh and English, and an English-born English-speaking father who never mastered any of the Welsh language, other than to understand phrases. But following the death of my mother when I was very young and my sister was just six-weeks old, my father and I went to live with an uncle and aunt; both were Welsh-speaking and their son was a pure Welsh speaker. My uncle and aunt became my mother and second father but I always distinguished between 'Owa', as I called my uncle, and my father whom I called Dad. Two languages persisted in my home and I recall how Mam and Owa switched to English, out of respect, when, in late afternoon, my Dad came home from work. My cousin/brother, D. T. Williams, was by this time away at college and his arrival home at holiday times was a signal for further confusion; he spoke Welsh to his parents and English to my father and to me.

I recall that the house was always full of books. My mother constantly read Dickens in winter months and would switch to more lighthearted 'novel' books at other times. There was Zane Grey and journals relating to sporting activities, together with John O' London, John Bull and the ubiquitous *Daily Herald*. Thus I learned to read in English. Mine was a home full of culture (a piano appeared), but the medium was English not Welsh. Proximity to a Welsh-speaking grandmother would appear to have ensured that my use of Welsh would be a constant and continuous feature. In practice, I was bilingual to the age of five, but by the time I had reached the grammar school, at the age of eleven, although my understanding of Welsh was good, my use of it was non-existent. I know that my young life was enriched by my hearing conversation about wide-ranging topics flavoured by a special sense of humour that I have since come to understand as belonging to Rhymney. D. T. Williams later produced *My People's Ways* about Rhymney and its inhabitants. The very title of this work clearly suggests what the writer was describing; it was singularly a description of a Welsh way of life.

During all this time I had been a regular attender at a Welsh chapel and gone to a Welsh Sunday School. The major issue, I think, in determining my consciousness of being a Welshman is that I grew up in Wales, that I was surrounded by institutions which were Welsh, and that the historiography of Rhymney as a community had to do with an identifying of Welshness in all of us. This was irrespective of religious background or use of mother-tongue. Our involvement in the community at large seemed to pre-determine that we could become Welshmen and Welshwomen without even considering that we needed to communicate in any language other than English.

I have to accept, when attempting to make a statement about claims to be Welsh, that in many ways we were Welsh because we were told that we were Welsh. Despite the English surname that I bear, I was for some reason accepted as Welsh. My sister who lived quite close by with another uncle-and-aunt/mammy-and-daddy-and-cousin/sister, in identical circumstances, must have found herself in the same situation.

As I look back upon family structure, I am reminded that the society in which I grew was essentially matriarchal, and it was my aunt/mother who guided my behaviour, education and involvement to a large degree in what went on in the chapel. The chapel, which was a Welsh Baptist chapel, full of strong men-deacons, a wonderful minister in G. R. M. Lloyd, gifted women, good singers and excellent social arrangements, dominated my life. My aunt imbued me with an interest in literature, always through the medium of English, a love of music and a need to join in things that were musical. I have to say that any success I had came from the determination of the females in my family that I should succeed, if only as a tribute to my mother who had been their youngest sister and had demonstrated certain academic abilities throughout her life. The fact that she had been unable to afford to take up a place in a grammar school but had become a shop assistant in a very high-quality local drapers' was a sufficient indication of her prowess. For me, however, the drive was towards a good matriculation and ultimately some kind of college training. That I aspired to this is largely attributable to the power and influence of a Welsh family and its persuasiveness in convincing me that there was no other direction in which I was to go. The drive to education was a Welsh characteristic.

On the male side, the talk was of sporting events, usually associated with the activities of the Welsh XV, though there was great interest in boxing, and visits to the booths where Tommy Farr and the Moody Brothers performed were often described. Soccer was never ignored; and there was a keen interest in the doings of Bradman and Jardine and 'young' Len Hutton. My father, who was born in Staffordshire and finally raised in the village of Abercanaid near Merthyr Tydfil, went to the First World War, was wounded, and emerged in 1918 physically strong enough to become a professional soccer player. He had the common sense to train himself as an electrician, and combined two careers for a number of years until the death of my mother. His was the gift of physical strength and prowess which, somehow, my young mind associated with all the other names one heard at home—Wilfred Wooller, Claude Davey, Haydn Tanner, who were rugby players of Welsh origin—but none of them matched my father's fame as far as I was concerned. For many years I was called 'Harry Askey the footballer's son', and I felt that somehow or other I had to aspire to some success in this particular field.

My maternal grandfather did not exist in my life for he died before my birth. Tom Jenkins was a man of great stature in the community. He was a man who had started working at the age of nine in the local clay-level. He spoke very little English and learned to read in the local Sunday School but through the medium of Welsh. This gentleman was lionized in the family and, indeed, must have been a considerable figure; he learned to speak and write English, and finally became a check-weigher in one of the local collieries. This was the person who weighed the amount of coal that colliers had cut and for which they were paid. All working men around him placed their total trust in him because he safeguarded their income and their well being. Tom Jenkins also became interested in local politics and was one of the first Liberal/Labour councillors in the Rhymney valley. He was struck down by diabetes and died at an early age in his mid forties, just at that point in time when he might have been adopted as a candidate for Parliament. His acceptance into Westminster in these very stirring years at the turn of the century would have set him up and would have been a true recognition of his great worth. He was Welsh. I often think what I would have felt like if my grandfather had indeed become a Member of Parliament; my own efforts to succeed would have been all the more worthwhile.

The association of my family with the area of radical politics is something that continued for three generations. Sadly, the family did not achieve instant fame, but there seemed to me always to be someone who was aspiring to the local council, who was serving on committees, was in the choir or who set himself up to write books. The socio-political features of my home town were indelibly printed on me in my growing up. I knew Idris Davies, and although he was a generation ahead of me, he seemed to me to embody all those things that the people in my background would have recognised as great. His poetry was about the Wales in which I grew up.

153

Princetown, Ogmore Valley, by David Bailey

I followed my father into the world of soccer; not a very respected activity to pursue because many people seemed set to regard soccer as a second-best choice. Whatever activity one followed as a young person, you were seen as a native of Rhymney and you hoped that the town was proud of you. It did not matter what your achievements were as long as they set you apart from the crowd. It seems a characteristic of all of us who are Welsh that we love to pick out an individual, and although he may have no honour in his own patch he is accorded respect provided those in other patches honour him.

When considering Welshness in relation to me as a person, I have to consider that much of my background reflected the great developments that had taken place over the previous century. Both my grandparents were confirmed Nonconformist Welsh-speakers who had learned to read in the late nineteenth-century drive to literacy. The movement in the late nineteenth century towards political awareness in south Wales was certainly mirrored in the way that my grandparents came to the forefront. At the same time there was never any question that the first loyalty of parents, uncles and aunts lay with the chapel and all it stood for. This is equally true of much of the rest of Britain—but all I can say is that it was different in Rhymney as in Wales generally.

As a seventeen-year old going to University College, Aberystwyth, I was fortunate enough to be placed in 'digs' with three other young men who had similar backgrounds to my own in terms of geography but were dissimilar in terms of 'personal' location. We were welded together into a group of friends by our landlady, Miss Jones. My recollection is that Miss Jones would have been a lady in her late sixties whose life had bridged the two centuries. She was a spinster whose father and brothers were seafarers. She was a pillar of Christianity and displayed all the solid virtues of kindness and loyalty that persuaded her to dedicate her life to the nurturing of young men students whose records and achievements were very dear to her. I would have said that she was politically conservative with a strong leaning to liberalism, but, at the same time, had a great admiration for private achievement and enterprise. She chose to spend the last fifteen or twenty years largely within the confines of her own home. She relied upon her friends to visit her and it was from these friends that she gathered the news and gossip of the day. The sources of information were very varied but included bus conductors, who travelled on the country buses; marketeers, who mixed with local farmers; and sundry others who frequented various places of worship. The house was called 'Brooklyn' and overlooked the harbour at Aberystwyth; no doubt the name was derived from the sea-going

155

journeys of her father and brother. Ironically, it is now called 'Folkestone'. Miss Jones' influence on me was immeasurably good. She would not have attempted to influence where we went or what we ultimately did, but we knew we had to succeed. Miss Jones was unmistakably Welsh.

It is easy to hide behind one's background when considering what one is: for example, to blame one's own uncertainty on one's formative environment. Reflecting on my time spent in England, I am certain that I took a risk transposing the young man I was from the Welsh country-side to London. I feel more at home in Wales than I do in England, although I have many good friends across the border. Being anxious to communicate and perhaps over-anxious to please, I may in the past have lost the admiration of people who are essentially English since I do not have the reserve to be able to cope with their cooler, less quick or volatile approach. I am certain that communicating with people and the ability to do so at all levels is a great feature of the Welshman whether by the written or the spoken word. I do not think the gift is related solely to scholarship, although it does depend upon a vocabulary achieved by practice, good hearing and careful listening. I think that in Wales those of us who are not just garrulous but who wish to speak have a better chance of being listened to than in many other parts of the United Kingdom.

Over the past forty years I have read a great deal of work by Anglo-Welsh writers and, since my improved Welsh has allowed me to do so, the works of contemporary Welsh writers. It appears to me that literature in Wales and about Welshmen seems on the whole to be full of sparkling generalisations. The writer always seems to have grasped the *genius loci* and to present people as they are.

There is a great division between what one may call upland and lowland Britain. If Britain had been all lowland each successive invasion would have rapidly overrun the whole island so that there would have been no discernible difference between what we now call Celtic Britain, in Wales and Scotland, and the Saxon districts which lie to the east. The truth is that our uplands discouraged invaders or at least held them at bay, and the Saxons certainly made little progress into Wales. This is not to say that there were not considerable overlaps in the settlement of what is now Wales but each flood or influx came sufficiently long after its predecessor to allow for general assimilation. Wales was never completely Romanised and life amongst the Welsh remained tribal. The Normans made very little impression other than around the coasts. Thus it was in these upland areas, Welsh customs prevailed and the language survived.

Today that language still survives and, indeed, is beginning to show evidence of re-establishing itself in areas of Wales that were heavily anglicised. The progress is slow but follows a determined path and it would appear that it owes a great deal to the determination and solidity of the native inhabitants. Those who stand in the west and look east must do so with a certain sense of pride at having withstood incursion and having retained an independence of outlook.

How does one distinguish an Englishman from a Welshman? I think that neither Englishman nor Welshman can tell us because to do so would require an objectivity of outlook which is probably beyond the capability of human beings. What I am certain about is that the person who will eventually arrive at a satisfactory definition is one who knows both languages. In the context of my own life, the fact that I was able to understand Welsh has determined a number of developments that I would not have otherwise countenanced. Certainly the language has given me a confidence to live in Wales. It is said that the best Welshman is the one that lives out of Wales: this I can deny.

'WELSH BY PROXY'
Neil Caldwell

How can I describe my feelings for Wales and the Welsh? It is so difficult for me to sum up why I have stayed so long in this land, that I would rather not face the task for fear it will be too revealing. As in love, I prefer to do rather than to say, believing my actions will convey my inner feelings, though I know it to be an inadequate response. On this occasion, however, I am tempted by a desire to appear in print, to wallow in nostalgia and otherwise indulge myself.

My path to understanding Welshness probably began in 1970 when I arrived as a bright-eyed student in Aberystwyth. It could be traced back further to the affinity I had for the social values of the north of England, and perhaps even Scotland, on my father's side. Suspecting this to be little more than romantic nonsense, it could equally have its origins in our holidays in Wales, especially Dolwyddelan, where I was taken by old Mr. Pierce of Bryntirion farm to see the local team play Penmachno. I can still recall the tea which followed in the homely farmhouse, with the high mantelpiece lined with trophies from many a sheepdog trial.

As a child I felt alienated from the prosperous society of the south-east which, in my native Buckinghamshire at least, was already overwhelming the local rural culture. I did not possess the experience to rationalise my feelings then, and in any case, as an emigrant from London (at the age of three), I was also part of this unstoppable phenomenon called 'progress'. A brief and unsuccessful spell in private education was followed by a much happier time at Chenies, a traditional, rural primary school whose playground echoed to the sound of the local Buckinghamshire dialect. Nine years later I left the boys-only grammar school to complete my education in Wales, at Aberystwyth, where my great grandfather had once served with the local militia.

I was not a willing recruit to the University of Wales, having set my heart on Lancaster, and I took time to adjust. Crossed in love also, and sentenced to endless nights of sleeplessness in a basement room of the Manora Hotel, listening to the snoring of a clergyman's son from Haverfordwest, I thought there was no hope. But a year's recuperation in lodgings provided by dear Miss James of Hendre Gwyndir, Bow Street, brought me to my senses. A few passionate encounters with the local Welsh girls also contributed!

Though never 'in hall', in the residential sense, I enjoyed being part of a close-knit community, even if I was always careful to ensure I could escape to solitary and contemplative peace. This contradictory desire to be in the thick of things, and yet to stand apart from the crowd, I have discovered to be an indelible feature of my personality. My student days culminated in a Union career which was my passport to the privileges of power. In many ways this was the turning point on which so much of my future life would depend.

My partner in the Students' Union was a lovable rogue from Bangor. At first we loathed the sight of each other, since we were the products of very different cultures. Within a month, however, we were the best of friends, which was just as well because I became my fellow-sabbatical's personal chauffeur for the year, after he lost his licence. It was he who knocked the edges of this Sassenach, exposing me unmercifully to the brutal force of radical Welsh politics. Before long he became known in certain circles as the 'North Walian Brigand' and I, his 'Saxon Pet'!

Although a fighter by nature, I offered no resistance to this onslaught which was only thinly diluted with humour. In truth, I was fascinated by my encounter with the 'real' Welsh, having only met the anglicised kind before. I found I could identify with their cause, even though their methods were so unsporting! During that year, and the few which followed, I chose to bear the penalty for being English in the hope that I might learn what it was to be Welsh. Having lost my roots in England, I was intoxicated by a culture which had such strong links with its past.

How proud I was, therefore, to be physically removed from the Rhyd holiday-homes trial in Blaenau Ffestiniog and stand, silent, outside in the bitter cold with Ffred Ffrancis. How thrilled to be asked to drive on a night mission to destroy English-only roadsigns. How flattered to find myself in the company of the Free Wales Army! This was real life, not the superficial kind I had left in the cocktail belt of Chalfont St. Peters, Buckinghamshire, and I was beginning to feel part of it. The zeal of the convert was apparent, and there was no stopping me.

It should be noted that despite all this partisan activity, I could not speak nor barely understand a word of Welsh. My support for the cause was purely theoretical, though emotionally felt. I have recognised this feeling in many who are on the edge of Welsh-speaking society and yet want to take the plunge. At this stage you are still an onlooker, and in that sense ephemeral. Imagine my fear, therefore, when at one point I was deposed from power in the Union and had to face the prospect of returning to my native land. How could I possibly return? No one in England would ever understand how I felt or what I'd been through.

The only answer was to commit myself even more fully to Wales. Indeed, the longer I stayed the more I found I wanted to know about this schizophrenic society. Over the last fifteen years, I have lived in Aberystwyth, Pontypridd, Abertawe, Aberdaron and lately in Llanfair Caereinion. I married a lovely, loyal Swansea girl with roots in Llŷn and all the cultural credentials I could have wished for. We have two children, Catrin and Owain, who know their country from one end to the other, though they'd dearly love to stay in one place for a while! I am certainly much the wiser for this experience and can at last speak Welsh. Let me explain how I did it.

As you now appreciate, my understanding of Wales as a nation far outstripped my knowledge of its language, superficial though that understanding was. Of course, I gave all the classic excuses for not learning Welsh: well, everyone understands English, don't they?; I'm not a linguist, I was appalling at French in school; I haven't got time; in any case no one ever speaks Welsh to you even if you learn, and so on. These are nothing but excuses which reveal a basic lack of commitment. Until they are exorcised, no real progress can be made.

Like so many others, I began by attending an evening class. It was difficult to believe I would ever be fluent under this regime which seemed to cater only for the mildly interested. We would spend at least half our time each week chatting (in English) about the peculiarities of Welsh grammatical forms. That, and the weather. Still, it salved my conscience and satisfied my wife that I was trying. Being an all-or-nothing type, it didn't satisfy me.

So I cleared the decks and signed up for an intensive ten-week Wlpan Course at the *Urdd* Centre in Cardiff, under the irrepressible Gwilym Roberts. The strange thing was that, although this involved a total commitment of three hours a night, five nights a week, it was far easier and a great deal more fun than the once-a-week evening class. For a start I knew every evening was filled, so that my days were arranged to suit. I was immersed in the language to such a degree that it would whirl in my head during the day. On top of this, I got to know my disparate group of learners so well that we lost all inhibitions and fell about laughing at the least excuse! It was wonderful.

It was also very effective because it concentrated on the spoken language, rather than grammatical forms. I found I could at last make myself vaguely understood in Welsh, though I recall entering a pub in Porthmadog, confidently ordering a half of bitter, and then being told it cost *un ar hugain* when I was expecting something like *dauddeg un*. I left with my tail between my legs having been lightly dismissed as a *dysgwr*, a learner. Obviously not known for their sympathetic attitude towards learners—the Porthmadog *rafins*!

Unshaken by this experience I set about murdering the language of heaven at every opportunity. I soon discovered, however, that outside the confines of *Canolfan yr Urdd* there were few opportunities to be had. Although my wife was part of a thriving Welsh community of young mothers, I remained on the fringes unable or unwilling to plunge headlong into the bubbling, ghetto culture of Welsh-speaking south Wales. With two small children already making themselves understood in their native tongue, I knew I had another important decision to make if I was ever really going to speak the language. The opportunity soon appeared in the form of two quite extraordinary jobs with the National Trust, in Llŷn.

Within a few months we had exchanged our young, urban, upwardly-mobile existence on an estate near Pontypridd, for the untamed, windswept beauty of Llŷn. It was a career move which left our friends aghast. I became the Trust's first countryside warden on the peninsula, while Betsan became the curator of Plas yn Rhiw, an idyllic small manor house perched on a wooded ledge above Porth Neigwl (Hell's Mouth Bay). There followed three of the most pleasurable years of my life, helping to conserve the house and estate, getting to know at least some of the local characters (and there are many!), and living what for me was a refreshingly simple lifestyle. I had time to chat and get to know people, the children were growing up monoglot Welsh, and as a family we were welcomed into this most Welsh of communities.

From Llŷn we moved to Gower, another peninsula, but that is as far as the similarity goes. Culturally and linguistically the contrast is stark, as Gower, like south Pembrokeshire, has been a peculiarly anglicised enclave for many hundreds of years. Its richness of soil, wildlife and landscape was striking, as was the wealthy sophistication of its new settlers from Swansea and further afield. A diminishing circle of old Gower folk still held sway over the extensive common lands and productive coastal farms, and provided the greatest challenge for a countryside warden.

Another contrast was having to live in Swansea itself to ensure our children could continue to enjoy a Welsh-medium education. One of the most difficult decisions was to remove Catrin and Owain from Aberdaron's vibrant and delightful Crud y Werin School, and put them in distinctly urban Bryn y Môr School in Brynmill. Being practically monoglot Welsh, Owain had an unhappy time trying to make himself understood. However, he eventually discovered that a knowledge of English was the key to success, and he now speaks a strange form of Americanized Welsh, and is the bane of our lives!

These days we live in Llanfair Caereinion, tucked away in the rolling hills of Montgomeryshire. From the heart of Wales, I reflect on our wanderings and sustain my contact with the varied communities of Wales through a fascinating job. However, I am uncertain whether my appointment as Director of Wales' premier countryside campaigner is just a sad reflection of its underlying anglicisation, or a mark of my transformation into a kind of Welshman by proxy; probably a bit of both. Certainly, there is no doubt in my own mind that I have absorbed a great deal that is distinctly Welsh over the last nineteen years, but it is also clear to me that I can never be truly Welsh.

For a start, I display the emotional detachment and calculated organisational skills of the colonial administrator. I never contemplate any action without prior analysis and sound preparation. Travelling in hope is not good enough for me; I want to know exactly where I am going and how I am going to get there. I am not one for a spontaneous uprising against injustice, but rather a determined, well-planned resistance which aims to beat the opposition at its own game. I also like plain speaking which, though it may upset some, is preferable to saying only what people want to hear. I cannot recognise my traits as Celtic in origin, though I am strongly attracted to the emotional spontaneity of both the Celtic and Latin temperament. The attraction of opposites it seems.

Whilst a knowledge of Welsh is the key to a deeper understanding of Wales, it is also a means to an end. My schooldays were spent studying the literature and history of England (not that much of it stuck), so that I possess little more than a superficial appreciation of the rich historical, cultural and religious foundations of Welsh society. So my key, such as it is, will only ever open the door a fraction of the way. Despite this, what I do see convinces me how vital it is that the people of Wales remain firmly in possession of their cultural and historical roots. Without this extensive and supportive network of traditions, any new growth will prove fragile indeed.

There is obviously still much to be done to secure a future for the language, not that it can ever be guaranteed. Legislation may help, though it depends fundamentally on the attitudes of those who speak it, as well as those who do not. Those attitudes have changed quite dramatically over the last twenty-five years. Welsh is no longer seen as a symbol of backwardness, but increasingly as an essential prerequisite for success, in Wales at least. I very much hope that both tolerance and creativity will characterise a more fully bilingual society, in which the slavish translation of forms and reports is only a minor element of an otherwise rich and varied culture. Some things can truly only be said and done in Welsh; as is also the case with English and every other language. It is clear to me that if people want to participate in a society at anything more than a superficial level, then they must make an effort to learn the language. There really is no other way.

My particular journey to this truth seems to have turned me into a cultural hybrid. I shout my support for Wales on the rugby pitch, but I tune to Radio 4. I accept the need for linguistic ghettos, but I want to be part of a wider, multicultural society. I feel people should have the right to educate their children through the medium of Welsh, and that Welsh should be more widely required for work in Wales, but would never wish to restrict people's chances of broadening their horizons in England or elsewhere in the world, just as mine were broadened on coming to Wales. There is no future in isolation, so the task must be to build a culturally secure, self-confident society in Wales that can usefully compete in, and contribute to, the wider world. If I can play a small part in that process I shall be very satisfied.

AT BALA
Joseph Clancy

It seethed beneath wind and rain
Last night, Ceridwen's cauldron;
Now, irresistible grace,
Llyn Tegid's been converted.
It has disappeared, assumed
Into the clear calm morning.

We could walk uphill across
Looking-glass land on branches
To the top, and hop a cloud
From Bala to Llanuwchllyn.
Instead, we stroll hand in hand,
Heading for nowhere special;
Sedate middle-aged lovers,
Spring harvest, we take our time.
We let the lakeside lead us
By green pastures where March lambs
Wobble to milk tranquil ewes.
Over a rise, past posted
Information on fishing,
Through a screen of yew our eyes
Are drawn to a small stone church,
A plot planted with headstones.

This might be any village
Churchyard whose stones speak Welsh
Posed for a picture postcard.
But the not uncommon names,
Thomas Charles, Lewis Edwards,
Pierce the placid morning's glass.
They kindle fire in the thatch
Of memory. At Bala
Christ was raised in sinfast hearts;
God's barefoot Word crossed mountain
And ocean with prints of flame
Struck glowing from this brazier.
The Arans and Arenigs
Rejoiced to leap in its light.

163

The great limbs shift in their sleep
Under cloudshade and sunlight.
We turn to walk the lakeside,
More scenery, now, than shrine,
Back to the town, clouds hover,
As hushed as a burnt-out heart.
A bush stirs. The breeze begins
To move upon the waters.

THE LAST LAUGH
Tony Bianchi

Siôn Gwilym eased his way through the crowded lounge and dropped the loose sheaves of manuscript on the bar.

'Only cash here, sir,' said the barman.

Siôn stared myopically, failing to get the joke. He bought his pint and retreated to the least crowded table. He'd been working his way through Lloyd's mammoth *Hanes Cymry Lerpwl* all morning and needed to finish another three chapters before calling it a day. The Press had a deadline to meet and Lloyd's idiosyncratic prose and shaky typing didn't help.

He'd just found his place in the 1860s when an elbow nudged his left side.

'That's Welsh, isn't it?'

Siôn nodded.

'You Welsh, then?'

Siôn smiled and waited for the inevitable.

'I'm Welsh, see—Splott born and bred, as they say—but not real Welsh like you. Don't have the language, see. Where you from, then? Somewhere up North?'

Siôn had faced this one before.

'A little village just outside Llanelli.'

'Aye, you can tell you're proper Welsh by the way you talks.'

Siôn downed his pint and decided that if he was to do any work he'd have to go back to the Press. He waved a self-conscious farewell and left.

Back at the Press, Siôn was more at home. He felt reassured by the heavy volumes of scholarship and the slimmer but still more precious collections of poetry which surrounded him. These, he knew, *were* the culture, *were* the nation, to which he belonged. He was so much luckier than the English, he thought, who didn't know who they were or where to find themselves. The whole of Wales—the *real* Wales—lay between these four walls. Siôn opened his arms wide to embrace it all.

By the end of the afternoon, Siôn's zeal had waned. He had a learner's class to take in three hours and there were still over forty pages of tortuous editing to complete. He decided to make tracks for home, take a shower and have a bite to eat. He hoped the evening's labours would seem less daunting on a full stomach. Siôn loped his way determinedly along the bleak city streets, until he entered the park by the tennis courts. Crossing the football pitches, he contended for right of way with a dozen or so yapping dogs. This always made him nervous. Their filth also angered him, so he was livid when at that moment a dog-owner allowed his charge to defecate in the midst of his intended path.

'Can't you keep your dog under control?' he snapped. 'People have got to walk this way, you know?'

The dog looked anxiously in both directions as the owner shouted back: 'They're only animals, you know. When they've got to go, they've got to go. There's tramps and all sorts doing it round here . . . go and tell them off. They should know better.'

'Yes, and so should you,' Siôn retorted. 'You're turning this park into an open sewer.'

The dog-owner moved menacingly close. 'And you're not even Welsh, either—you've no right to tell me what I do in my own city.'

This wrong-footed Siôn. Why should nationality have anything to do with dog-shit. Anyway, he *was* Welsh.

'*Ydych chi'n siarad Cymraeg, 'te?*'

The effect was instantaneous. The dog-owner faltered and stared nervously at the ground.

'Er . . . er . . . *ydy, er, nac ydy* . . . *Tipyn bach* . . . that's right, isn't it?' He looked up and simpered apologetically.

'Not done it since I was in school, see.'

Siôn laughed and walked off in triumph.

The Welsh class was always a testing experience. It demanded a quick wit and a gregarious spirit which Siôn found it hard to muster. However, even this city was, he supposed, part of the *gwinllan a roddwyd* and it was his duty to help shepherd the flock back into the fold. If *he* didn't give the poor sods a chance to re-discover the Welshness they'd lost, who would? He kept gnawing at this thought as his pupils began to amble in.

Old Mrs. Grover was the first, as usual. She'd been learning Welsh for forty years, on and off, God help her, and still looked shocked when anybody tried to speak to her in the language.

'*Noswaith dda, Mrs. Grover. Shwd ŷch chi heno?*'

'*Er, da iawn, diolch.* Very nippy tonight, isn't it? Think I'll keep my coat on.'

She settled down near the radiator and beamed at Siôn in anticipation of an entertaining evening. Mary-Ellen and Brett sat down next to her. She was American and he English, but having decided that a Welsh-medium education would be a good thing for their daughter, they'd taken the plunge themselves. Six months of Welsh behind them and there wasn't a word of English in the house. If anything vindicated Siôn's mission, this was it.

'*Fi gyda annwyd heno, Siôn,*' piped up Mary Ellen enthusiastically, '*achos rydw i wedi mynd allan yn y glaw, er, nos diwethaf.*'

Siôn groaned inwardly: they'd been taking lessons from their daughter again. He had a brief, grotesque vision of them trying to make love in this gobbledygook. Still, he thought, they were making tremendous progress —if only all his pupils were so committed. Siôn mumbled some words of sympathy before getting ready to start the lesson.

There were eleven in the class. Only two of them were Welsh—Mrs. Grover and Malcolm, a young chap from up the Valleys who'd been a miner before the closures. Siôn felt unsure of him. He knew the cause of the language needed more of his kind if it was to have a major impact in these parts. But he was torn between the desire to save him from his cultural disinheritance and a nagging feeling that Malcolm would never, however hard he tried, really belong to Siôn's Wales. Why did he want to learn Welsh, anyway? This was the puzzling question. Now Geoffrey had an obvious motivation—he'd got a researcher's job on the radio and wanted to improve his career prospects. Per, the Breton, needed the language to help him with his comparative study of nineteenth-century Breton and Welsh literature. And the rest—well, to be honest, they had good intentions and liked the night out, the company and the vague promise of a new world which at present they could only glimpse half-comprehendingly in their television screens.

Siôn had recorded an episode of *Pobl y Cwm* to show to his pupils. It exposed them to north Walian and south Walian Welsh and presented the kinds of situation in which, he supposed, they might some day find themselves. It would also allow him to reminisce about life in the Welsh heartland and extol the virtues of community and tradition: this always drew a sympathetic, even envious response from his pupils.

166

The video began with a scene in the Deri Arms. After a minute or two, Siôn pressed the pause button and explained some of the colloquialisms with which the class was unlikely to be familiar.

'*Dim ond yn y de, wrth gwrs, y byddwch yn clywed yr ymadrodd "hala fe mas". Yn y gogledd . . .* '

Mary Ellen looked a little worried.

'But *we* live in the south,' she protested, 'and that's not what our Laura learns at school. Why can't they all speak the same? Don't those guys at the BBC know that learners like us are the only future the language has got? Isn't it their job to make programmes *we* can understand?'

Siôn tried to explain that the series had to be realistic or Welsh speakers wouldn't find it credible. 'Back home in my village, you see . . .' This time it was Malcolm who interrupted.

'You can't call that realistic. I've been over west Wales lots and there's nowhere like that. That Deri Arms is a con. It's all Brummies own the pubs nowadays and half the people who drink there don't speak Welsh. And them that do haven't got much time for the likes of us—not that we'd understand them, anyway.'

'Well, that's your fault then, old chap, isn't it?' Brett chipped in.

Eleven perplexed faces turned in his direction, demanding an explanation but fearful of what might follow.

'I mean to say, with due respect and all that, if you chaps from the Valleys hadn't sold your birthright, then you wouldn't be in this pickle now, would you?'

He looked around for some sign of approval, but it was too late to turn back.

'And anyway, you can't come that anti-English malarkey with me. You need the likes of us here, because we've got more respect for your culture than you have yourselves. In fact, I'm doing you a very big favour by learning your language—I don't need to, you know.'

Malcolm had had enough.

'Then you can stuff your bloody favours, butty, 'cos it's not my bloody language anyway. And if this is the future of the Welsh language—you load of wankers dreaming about making good in the Deri fucking Arms—then I'm getting out now before I'm certified.'

He turned to Siôn. 'When I came here, I thought I was going to learn something that would help me make sense of the place I lived in. And what did I get? A bunch of arse-lickers on the make, academic nutters, middle-class hippies, and the rest too bloody naïve to realise they're being conned. I know you're doing your best, mate—it's your language and you've got to fight for it.' He looked derisively around the class. 'But not with these buggers.'

Malcolm left the room. Siôn had half a mind to end the misery there and then, but was surprised at the air of relief which had suddenly descended on the class. Mrs. Grover summed up the general mood.

'Good riddance, I say. And I hope his mother washes his mouth out with soap and water when he gets home.'

Cadwn y ffynnon rhag y baw, thought Siôn as he pressed the play button on the video recorder. All sat forward and concentrated on the screen with new intensity.

Siôn finished editing the Lloyd manuscript at ten o'clock the next morning. He could now put his feet up for a couple of hours before checking through the final proofs of the new press catalogue. But as luck would have it, no sooner had he sat down with his coffee and digestives than in walked the boss, Ifor Hywel.

'Sorry to bother you, Siôn,' he said, 'I can see you are busy. I wondered, actually, whether you might do me a little favour this evening?'

Ifor spoke Welsh with a mincing, pedantic correctness which Siôn assumed was a necessary qualification for the job. It was a trait he had already begun to affect but which at the same time increased his sense of awkwardness and inarticulacy. He stammered an ingratiating reply.

'Er, certainly, Ifor. I'd, er, I'd be delighted to be of assistance . . . tonight, you said?'

'Yes, that's it. I should very much appreciate your standing in for me at this reception down at the Exchange . . .'

'Ah, Dafydd Guto's book, you mean—the one set in Llŷn that they've dramatised for television.'

'*Yn union.*'

The Press had published Dafydd Guto's first novel the previous year. It was one of those works of rural nostalgia which they were going in for so much these days. An independent production company had snapped it up, decked it out in period crinolines and clogs, and were now to give the public a first taste of the resulting confection at the company's base in the old Coal Exchange. Siôn was not blind to the incongruousness of it all. He reflected, however, that as long as the links were being made— as long as the values of the tradition were being transmitted—then the end justified the means. Guto's book did, after all, look perfectly at home on his bookshelf between W. J. Gruffydd's *Hen Atgofion* and the poems of Isfoel. And it would become, in time, part of the same canon—that tradition which for centuries had held Wales together despite all the forces of dissolution which were ranged against her. Yes, he was looking forward to meeting Mr. Guto. He pulled the book down from the shelf. A fine cover, thought Siôn, but rather sketchy biographical details: '. . . a descendant of the Rev. John Elias . . . family has lived in Llŷn for generations . . . remarkable debut . . .' Perhaps he'd discover more about the author's background this evening.

Siôn was amongst the first to arrive. Although he disliked the awkward preambles to these occasions—the introductions, the obsessive prying into family histories—these were the people with whom he felt most at home. They shared a common concern with *y pethe*—they could exchange anecdotes about the last eisteddfod, speculate on who would be appointed to the vacant chair, rail at the appalling standard of Welsh on S4C and lament the passing of yet another irreplaceable guardian of the tradition. Yes, that was it: what held them together was the knowledge that they and they alone could cherish and foster that tradition. At least, with them, Welsh literature would *remain* Welsh literature: an inviolate pearl, even if all else turned to dross.

Amidst the array of professors, preachers, poets, producers and publishing apparatchiks like himself, Siôn could not as yet pick out the author. He walked slowly around the panelled room, looking for an unfamiliar face. A hand tapped his shoulder.

'John, me old mate . . .'

Siôn turned in panic. A bearded face smiled at him. No, this was no one he knew, he was fairly sure of that. And yet the voice seemed so familiar—and speaking English, too.

'Er, hello . . . I'm sorry, have we met?'

'Have we met! John, you remember me . . . your old china . . . Southgate High . . . White Hart Lane on a Saturday afternoon . . . Wednesday night at the Folk Club . . . Dave Corbet. Doesn't it ring a bell?'

Siôn had broken out in a cold sweat.

'Or should I say, Dave Corbett, alias Dafydd Guto . . . *ers i mi droi'n Gymro!*'

Siôn had not yet fully registered the broad north Walian accent when Sioned Williams, who'd directed the production, approached them.

'*Shw mae?* I didn't realise you two knew each other.'

'*Ydyn, 'tad,*' answered Dafydd. 'We've been mates since . . .'

'Er . . . since . . .' Siôn had to think of something quickly. 'Since the Llangefni Eisteddfod . . . *buon ni'n rhannu carafán, ontyfe,* Dafydd?'

169

'*Beth* . . .?' But the speeches were about to begin and Tom Eynon, head of Gwalia Productions, was calling for silence.

'. . . and what a tremendous achievement by a young man brought up in the bowels of the metropolis . . . the ancestral flame was rekindled on that foreign hearth . . . *ac y mae bellach wedi dychwelyd i fro ei gyndadau* . . . back to the land of his fathers. And what a debt we owe to those like Dafydd who learn the language and help keep our heartlands Welsh. And isn't it to the learners we must look now . . . *onid y dysgwyr a ddaw â gwaredigaeth i ni?* And now we can enjoy a preview of this moving film . . . a reminder of *y glendid a fu.*'

As the opening titles appeared on the screen, Dafydd grabbed Siôn by the arm and shunted him into one of the offices which adjoined the main room.

'*Beth yn y byd sy'n bod arnat ti,* John? What's all that nonsense about a caravan in Llangefni?'

Siôn whispered frantically: 'Listen, don't call me John, someone might hear. Siôn's my name . . .'

'Well, you might be Siôn now,' said Dafydd. 'And you've got a good west Walian accent to prove it. But that doesn't mean you're not John Thorpe of north London as well. Good God, man . . . What are you trying to hide?'

'Hide? I'm not hiding anything.' Somehow, Siôn's self-defence sounded less plausible, even to himself, when declared openly in this way. He went on nervously. 'I've left that life behind, Dave . . . er, Dafydd . . . I speak almost nothing but Welsh all day. I teach Welsh, I edit Welsh books for a living . . . I've even been fined for refusing to pay my TV licence. I *am* Welsh now, because . . . because I *feel* Welsh, it's as simple as that . . . and I don't want it all cluttered up with nonsense about some life in a nondescript suburb that I turned my back on years ago . . .'

'Well, well,' Dafydd reflected, with forced geniality. 'I'm full of admiration. A greater transformation could hardly be imagined. Shy London suburbanite turns Welsh extremist . . .'

'Oh, yes . . . you can mock . . . what about this then?' Siôn brandished Dafydd's book. '*Yr hen ragrithiwr!* You've done just the same yourself.'

'Ah, no! That's just where you are wrong, *gyfaill.*' Dafydd sat down and motioned to Siôn to do the same. He smiled and placed a friendly arm around Siôn's bowed shoulder.

'You see, Siôn,' explained Dafydd, 'amongst us lot, the English, there are basically two kinds of learner. I mean the real professional learner, not the dilettante, the dabbler, the "I'd better turn to English now I've got something important to say" brigade. Of these two kinds, you belong to the first. You're bored with bland, middle-class England, you go to university in Wales, probably because you can't get in anywhere else, and lo and behold, you discover an exotic other-world right on your own doorstep. And not only that, you find that you can acquire immediate citizenship of that world simply by learning its language. You can become ethnic overnight! And a freedom fighter to boot! How privileged and rooted you feel! How easily you satisfy that oh so English nostalgia for a more authentic, a more purposeful lifestyle. And in a little while you dress that self-importance in a cloak of elitist ideas drawn from this or that writer, so that you can justify looking down your nose at the deracinated masses you've left behind. There's only one drawback—going native means putting on an act . . . and you can be found out!'

Siôn was beside himself with indignation. '*Pa hawl sy gen ti*? . . . You've stitched together a whole genealogy to support your bogus claims to Welshness—John Elias, hill farmers in Llŷn, bloody Owain Glyndŵr as well, I shouldn't wonder . . .'

'Maybe, Siôn,' Dafydd said smugly. 'But there's no deceit involved. You see, I belong to the second and newer variety of professional learner —what I call the Thatcherite, or entrepreneurial learner. To me, the Welsh language, famous Welsh ancestors—and I do have them—*yr hen ffordd Gymreig o fyw*, and all that—they're all capital which I invest strategically to yield the maximum return. I exploit the cult of the learner to make inroads into my chosen market. I exploit the need of new Welsh elites to recruit where they can. And I'm completely open about it all. I bow before the sacred cows of Welshness, as you do, but whereas you conceal your Englishness, I eagerly confess mine. And I *mean* confess. Natives return all the time—but a sinner saved, an Englishman turned Welsh—that really appeals!'

Siôn had heard enough. 'You . . . you cynic. I'll . . . I'll . . .' But he was unable to say more. He rose from his chair and turned to leave. Dafydd called on him to wait.

'Just one last word, Siôn . . . Let's agree one thing before we part. I won't tell on you if you don't tell on me. We're in this together, O.K.? We both believe that being Welsh is a good career for an Englishman to follow these days, don't we? Otherwise, why the hell would we, old mates from Southgate High, N13, be talking Welsh together? Eh? That's a laugh, isn't it? Ha! That's really rich, that one. Ha, ha, ha . . .'

Dafydd Guto, alias David Corbett, had slipped into his native Cockney and continued to guffaw helplessly as Siôn made his way back

171

to the hall. There, the film had finished and the pundits were passing judgement. 'A work of genius.' 'It's remarkable how someone who has learned the language could understand . . .' 'At last, we have a writer who can take us into the twenty-first century.' Siôn took a glass of wine in his trembling hand and nodded enthusiastic agreement.

ACQUIRING AN INHERITANCE
Greg Hill

'Discovering that there is such a thing as Welshness has made me much more sharply aware of my Englishness.' That is a comment I collected while doing some background research on attitudes of English incomers to Wales for a magazine article I wrote a few years ago. It is my experience that it applies to many people who have come to Wales to live. In that sense living in Wales has enhanced their lives in a deeper way than has the change of physical environment they sought in coming here. At one time I might have left off the quotation marks and allowed the remark to describe my own experience. But as it stands the potential complacency it suggests requires some qualification to be made. Besides, I think I have changed a little since then.

So what about Welshness as a yardstick against which to measure other varieties of 'Britishness'? T. S. Eliot came close to defining the importance of the Welsh language entirely in terms of the survival of the idea of Englishness. But he spoke not as someone who had come to live in Wales, but as an American who had adopted both England and the English tradition as the basis of his overt cultural identity. He could see with the eyes of an outsider seeking a close engagement with the culture he wished to inhabit and, at the same time, as an alert cultural critic. For incomers to Wales from England the view of cultural reality may not be so clear. But for those who come to terms with the existence of a different tradition in Wales, and are therefore forced to assess their own relation to this, the idea of Welshness as a regional variety of Englishness ceases to make sense. For them it soon became obvious that moving to Wales is not like moving to Yorkshire or the West Country from London or Birmingham in spite of the superficial similarities in change of lifestyle which confronts anyone moving to a rural area from a city.

Some never see farther than that, experiencing the move to Dyfed or Gwynedd as a transition from city to country rather than from England to Wales. This is not to say they do not love Wales in their own way. Rather that they have no clear idea what it is that gives to it the aura of particularity which attracted them in the first place. I once met somebody who spoke enthusiastically about arriving at Pont Abraham services at the western end of the M4. Returning from visits to family in England, he felt that he was nearly 'home' when making a final refreshment stop at this point. For him Wales began where the M4 stops rather than when it crosses the Severn estuary. He seemed no more aware of being English, in the special sense suggested above, than he was aware of Welshness as anything other than a language he couldn't understand. He thought of himself simply as British. But those who become aware of the otherness of Wales have also taken a decisive step away from the notion of Britain as Greater England. Although this is a step many of the more sensitive among English incomers make, it is nonetheless one which does not always lead to a desire to integrate with or become part of that otherness. Like many an English expatriate before them, they are content to live 'abroad' nurturing their Englishness and using the native culture as something to define it against. Such an attitude demands some respect for things Welsh, but not a love of Welshness for its own sake.

That is the next step on the road and one which is much more difficult to take. Undoubtedly there is more than one way of taking it, but for me it was not possible even to be aware of the need to do this until I began learning Welsh. The language is often seen as the barrier that prevents English-speaking people from making the transition. But it can also be a way through the barrier. Learning Welsh allows an entry into Welsh life that would never be possible for someone moving to an English-speaking community in the Valleys. One might be made a welcome member of that community, but however hard one tried there would, I think, be a sense of something one did not quite have access to. In the Welsh-speaking areas learning the language can be a way of gaining that access. It is not, I should emphasise, in my view possible for an English person coming to Wales as an adult to abandon a sense of being English; nor do I think this is necessary. I have no doubt that children can do it, given the right schooling and a sufficiently enlightened attitude from their parents. I know a few English people who have become to all intents and purposes totally Welsh after coming here as university students and learning the language thoroughly. Whether they have lost all sense of being English is hard to assess. I certainly haven't, though

I waited until my mid twenties before coming to university here. Nor did I come with the specific intention of learning Welsh. This was something which grew out of my response to the cultural tensions I found here and of a sense of personal responsibility towards the culture of a country in which I had decided to live.

Like many of my left-leaning compatriots in the early 1970s I had always thought of myself as an internationalist who happened to live in London. Although my sense of being English was sharpened a little by a year in France, it was not until I came to Wales that I was able to see such internationalism as a convenient attitude for those secure in a sense of their own cultural superiority; able to wear their nationality lightly and even despise it without putting it under any threat. Paris at that time was full of Americans avoiding military service in Vietnam. My impression of how arrogantly American many of them were, even when they were denouncing all that their country stood for, perhaps enabled me to look at the possibility of a similar unconscious arrogance in my own Englishness. I certainly came to the conclusion that if we are able to be internationalists we need to know what it is we have to share and be prepared to take on board the aspirations of others. We need, too, to understand the protective feelings of those from cultures under threat and recognise the need for co-operation in diversity. In coming to live in Wales in the mid-1970s I felt I had entered a debate in which these issues were being addressed. That enabled me to begin assessing my own Englishness against a still hazy idea of Welshness. Engaging in this debate at the general level of theoretical discussion in the environment of a university was one thing. Resolving the issue of where I belonged was quite another. If roots were so important why didn't I go back and define my own? I am probably too close to those experiences to be able to analyse them accurately. I was aware of a positive sense of Englishness grounded in radical traditions, but also of ideal 'Englands of the mind' of which I could never be a part. There was also the lingering feeling that—for many in England—being English today does mean being British in the narrow imperialistic sense. If, like many others from England, I had mentally retreated from the ideology of Britishness, Wales was an ideal place to embody physically that retreat. On a less theoretical level, the community of my childhood no longer existed. The maze of back streets and tenements that I grew up in had been replaced by a large council estate. Much of the surrounding area was fast becoming what is now inner-London yuppie land. And the city is generally, a less pleasant place in which to live.

However complex the reasons, as I slowly learnt Welsh and began to interest myself in Welsh social and cultural issues, my sense of being a citizen, rather than merely an inhabitant, of Wales grew. I moved away from the Welsh-speaking west for a while to a teaching post in south Wales, but eventually managed to return to the Aberystwyth area where I could make sure that my children grew up in a Welsh-speaking community. This was particularly important as my wife, though Welsh, is not Welsh-speaking. My children now, therefore, speak English to their mother and Welsh to me. Bilingual families are becoming increasingly common in Wales and in some ways serve as a symbolic microcosm of the nation as a whole. To succeed they require patience and understanding and this reflects the qualities of positive toleration needed in the wider social sphere. Children, of course, simply regard the situation as perfectly natural. If anyone outside the family regards the phenomenon of an Englishman speaking Welsh to his children as odd, no one has ever made those feelings obvious. Some local friends say they are happy to regard me as Welsh. Certainly I consider myself to be a member of a Welsh community.

Becoming integrated into Welsh life has deepened my sense of what it is to be a human being, which, I think, is a general effect of coming to terms with any new dimension within the diversity of human cultures. It has given me access to a way of thinking, a language and a literature that I wouldn't otherwise have discovered. But these reasons, important though they are on a personal level, are peripheral to the central social issues that impelled me to find out about Welshness rather than just about Wales. The Welsh philosopher J. R. Jones spoke of a sense not of leaving his country but of his country leaving him. Many Welsh speakers have echoed that sentiment in finding themselves surrounded by people who have come to Wales to make a new life for themselves but have brought the culture of their old life with them. Welshness is a precious part of the inheritance of all the people of the island of Britain. Anyone who lives on this island has some responsibility to respect it. Those who live on the part of the island called Wales have a further duty to cherish it, wherever they feel they ultimately belong. I probably couldn't have written that if I didn't already feel that I belong in Wales. It is, by now, the only bit of 'home ground' I know. Acquiring a home is not simply acquiring land or property. The inheritance that goes with it cannot be bought for money. You have to work for it. You have to love certain things for their own sake. It takes time. But time couldn't be better spent.

CONTRIBUTORS

Phyllis Kinney was born in Pontiac, Michigan, USA. An opera fellowship at the Juilliard Graduate School of Music in New York was followed by two seasons as Principal Soprano with the Carl Rosa Opera Company in Britain. During this time she met and married Meredydd Evans, gave up opera and came to live in Wales. After a period in America, lecturing in music at a women's college, she returned to Wales where she has published several books of songs in Welsh for children; three books, jointly with Meredydd Evans, of Welsh traditional songs; and articles on Welsh traditional music. During the summer she organises academic courses for Americans who are interested in Welsh studies.

Sylvia Prys Jones was born in Sheffield in 1954. She attended school in Cardiff and later studied in Aberystwyth and Oxford, specializing in the field of modern Breton literature. She returned to Aberystwyth to work on the Welsh Dictionary.
   Sylvia Prys Jones now lives in Gwynedd, where she researches, teaches and translates.

A. M. Allchin is a Canon of Canterbury Cathedral and Director of the St. Theosevia Centre for Christian Spirituality in Oxford. He has written numerous books and articles on spirituality, and is the author of the volume on Ann Griffiths in the Writers of Wales series.

Jon Dressel was born in 1934 in St Louis, Missouri, and grew up in Granite City, Illinois, USA. He was educated in Chicago and St Louis, and was Assistant Professor of English at Webster University in St Louis from 1969 to 1976. He first came to Wales in 1961 and, in 1976, he established the Wales Study Centre for American students at Trinity College, Carmarthen, Dyfed.
   Jon Dressel has published two volumes of verse (*Hard Love and a Country*, 1977 and *Ianws Poems*, 1979).

John Geraint was born in mid-Rhondda in 1957. He was educated at Porth and the University of Oxford. He entered BBC Wales in 1978, and has since become a leading television producer. He has made a number of documentaries on Welsh social history, as well as programmes on India, Africa, the Middle-East and America. His portrayal of the after-effects of tragedy, *A Place like Hungerford*, was nominated by the Royal Television Society as best single documentary of 1988.

Patricia Elton Mayo was born in Brisbane, Australia, in 1915. She studied in Cambridge and Harvard. She has wide international experience in consultancy and management, and has worked in a number of positions within the

European Community. She is currently writing in the field of regional governments in Europe and European politics. Her publications include *The Roots of Identity* (1975) and *Sur l'Etat de L'Europe* (with Denis de Rougement and others, 1979).

Patricia Mayo is a member of the Welsh Union of Writers and holds the *Ordre des Palmes Academiques* (1956).

Gillian Clarke was born in Cardiff in 1937. From 1960 she has worked as a broadcaster, freelance writer and lecturer and, from 1975 to 1984, she was editor of the *Anglo-Welsh Review*. She is currently involved in the establishment of the Taliesin Trust, a centre for writers, at Llanystumdwy, Gwynedd.

Gillian Clarke has written a number of outstanding volumes of poetry, including *Selected Poems* (Carcanet, 1985) and her recent *Letting in the Rumour* (Carcanet, 1989), which won a Poetry Book Society recommendation.

Pennar Davies was born in Mountain Ash, Mid Glamorgan, in 1911. He has had a distinguished academic career, including periods of study at Cardiff, Oxford and Yale. His teaching career took him to Bangor, Brecon and finally to Swansea, where he was Principal and Professor of Church History at the Memorial College.

Pennar Davies has written three Welsh novels, two collections of short stories and three theological and other studies, but his reputation as a leading figure in Welsh cultural life is based chiefly on his several volumes of poetry. He is currently writing another novel (*Dyn Dihenydd*: 'Man of Doom'). His study of *E. Tegla Davies* in the Writers of Wales series is in English.

Meic Stephens was born in 1938 in Pontypridd, Mid Glamorgan. He was educated at the University College of Wales, Aberystwyth, graduating in French. He joined Plaid Cymru during his student days and stood as the party's election candidate in Merthyr Tydfil in the General Election of 1966. At the time a French teacher in Ebbw Vale, he was also among the first members of the Welsh Language Society, *Cymdeithas yr Iaith Gymraeg*. He began learning Welsh in the early 1960s, shortly before his marriage to a Welsh speaker; they have four children and Welsh is the language of their home. Between 1967 and 1990 Meic Stephens was Literature Director of the Welsh Arts Council.

Emyr Humphreys was born in 1919 in Prestatyn, Clwyd. He was educated at the University Colleges of Aberystwyth and Bangor, and has worked as a radio producer in Cardiff and as lecturer in drama at Bangor.

Emyr Humphreys has written many novels, and is the leading Welsh novelist (writing mainly in English) of his generation. In 1953 he won the Somerset Maugham Award, in 1959 the Hawthornden Prize, and in 1972, 1975 and 1979 the Welsh Arts Council Prize. He has also written several volumes of poetry, and his study *The Taliesin Tradition* has served as an introduction for many to the history of Welsh culture.

Raymond Garlick is an Anglo-Welsh poet and first editor of *The Anglo-Welsh Review*. His publications include *An Introduction to Anglo-Welsh Literature* (1972), *Anglo-Welsh Poetry 1480-1980* (1984) with Dr. Roland Mathias, *The Hymn to the Virgin* (1985), and seven books of poetry. His *Collected Poems 1946-86* was published in 1987, and his new collection of poems, *Travel Notes*, derived largely from recent visits to sites of antiquity in the Aegean, will be published in 1992.

Carl Iwan Clowes was born in Manchester of a Welsh mother and an English father. He is married to Dorothi, an Irish woman, and they have four children. He works as a Consultant in Public Health Medicine and part-time Consultant in Rural Development. Between 1974 and 1979 he was the Chairman of *Antur Aelhaearn*. He is the founder and Honorary President of the Nant Gwrtheyrn Trust. Since 1985 Carl Clowes has been Chairman of *Dolen Cymru*, Wales' link with Lesotho, and from 1988 has served as Chairman of the *Fforwm Iaith Genedlaethol* (National Language Forum). In 1979, 1983 and 1987, he was parliamentary candidate for Plaid Cymru.

R. S. Thomas was born in Cardiff in 1913. He was educated at University College, Bangor, and was ordained a priest of the Church in Wales in 1937. He has won the Welsh Arts Council premier award (1968), the Heinemann award of the Royal Society of Literature (1959) and the Queen's Gold Medal for Poetry (1964).
R. S. Thomas has won a world-wide reputation on the basis of his many volumes of verse, including his *Selected Poems* (1973) and his recent *The Echoes Return Slow* (1988).

Suzanne Greenslade was born in Atlanta, Georgia, USA, in 1952. She studied in America, and pursued her interest in languages in Spain, Italy and Japan. She married her Welsh husband in Tokyo in 1979, and moved to Wales in 1985. Suzanne Greenslade trained as a photographer and currently works as a full-time lecturer in photography at the West Glamorgan Institute of Higher Education in Swansea. She has two children.

Oliver Davies was born in 1956. He grew up in Swansea and Cardiff, and read Modern Languages at Oxford. After researching in the field of German literature, which took him for two years to the University of Cologne, he returned to Wales with his wife, Fiona Bowie. He now lives in Capel Curig, Gwynedd, and works as a freelance writer, translator and researcher. He is an Honorary Lecturer in the Department of Religious Studies at University College of North Wales, Bangor.

Zonia Bowen was born in the village of Ormesby St. Margaret, Norfolk, in 1926. She was educated in Yorkshire and at the University College of North Wales, Bangor. In 1947 she married Geraint Bowen, and taught in Wrexham, Clwyd.

In 1967 Zonia Bowen founded the Welsh women's movement *Merched y Wawr*, and from 1975 to 1980 she was Chair of the Welsh branch of the Killarney Pan-Celtic festival. From 1976 to 1986 she chaired the Welsh branch of the Celtic League. In 1984 she was guest lecturer in Breton at Ottowa University, Canada, and has published numerous books and articles. In 1981 she was made an honorary member of the Welsh Gorsedd of Bards.

Leigh Verill-Rhys was born in the United States where she taught creative writing for several years before moving to Wales. She is continuing to write and runs an expanding business, *Dalennau*, exporting Welsh books to the United States. She is a founding member of *Honno*, the Welsh Women's Press. Leigh Verill-Rhys is married to a Welsh musician and has three boys.

Jeffrey Gainer has been a priest of the Church in Wales since 1978. He is currently Lecturer in New Testament Studies at the University of Wales College of Cardiff and is Director of Pastoral Studies at St. Michael and All Angels Theological College, Llandaff.

Lena Rhys was born in Copenhagen in 1944. She trained as a teacher in Copenhagen before marrying Dai Arfon and moving to Wales in 1967. For the last five years Lena Rhys has worked as Project Secretary to the Social Work Practice Centre in Bangor, Gwynedd. She lives near Bethesda, and has two children, Olaf Llywelyn and Cynog Espen.

Ben Ridler was born in London in 1947. He was educated in Oxford, Bristol, and King's College, Cambridge. He did a research degree at Bristol University, followed by a year of teaching in London.

In 1972 he moved to Llanfachreth, near Dolgellau in north Wales. Ben Ridler is currently a Lecturer in Communications at Coleg Meirionnydd, Dolgellau, Gwynedd, and also teaches music to the adult mentally-handicapped.

Pat Neill retired in 1980 to a smallholding in Llannarth, Dyfed, after a career in teaching. He writes poetry, prose and music, and has been successful in both local and national eisteddfodau. He is a member of *Talwrn y Beirdd*.

Tony Conran was born in India in 1931. He is a leading Anglo-Welsh poet, and has published in addition numerous translations of Welsh poems, including *The Penguin Book of Welsh Verse*. The most recent volume of his own work is *Blodeuwedd* (1988).

Bobi Jones was born in Cardiff in 1929. He was educated in Cardiff and Dublin. After a period of teaching, he lectured in Education before switching to the Welsh Department, eventually becoming Professor of Welsh at Aberystwyth.

Bobi Jones is an enormously prolific Welsh writer and thinker, whose many volumes of poetry and prose, criticism and scholarship have earned him a leading position in Welsh cultural life. His *Selected Poems* have recently appeared in English translation.

John Barnie was born in Abergavenny, Gwent, in 1941. He was educated in Abergavenny and Birmingham University. Between 1969 and 1982 he was Lecturer in English at the University of Copenhagen. Since 1985 he has worked as co-editor of the magazine *Planet*. He has published three collections of poems (*Borderland*, 1984; *Lightning Country*, 1987; *Clay*, 1989) as well as a collection of essays (*The King of Ashes*, 1989). His most recent work, *The Confirmation*, was published in 1992.

Noragh Jones was born in the north of Ireland and studied at Trinity College, Dublin. She worked and lived in the south of Ireland as a librarian until she was thirty. She lectured in Management at Leeds Polytechnic and did her Ph.D. in Management Education at Bradford University. She now researches and writes on feminist theology, and teaches an evening class on 'Women and Religion' in Aberystwyth. She is married with a daughter.

Daniel Mullins was born in County Limerick, Ireland, in 1929. He was educated in Ireland, at St. Mary's College, Aberystwyth, Oscott College and University College, Cardiff. He is an Honorary Fellow of St David's University College, Lampeter.

Daniel Mullins was ordained priest in 1953. In 1970 he became Auxiliary Bishop, and in 1987 was translated to the See of Menevia. The Rt. Rev. Daniel Mullins is chairman of the Committee for Catholic Education and Formation, and is a Member of Court at the University College, Cardiff.

Fiona Bowie was born in 1956 and was brought up in Surrey. After completing a degree in Anthropology at Durham University, she did a doctorate in Social Anthropology in Oxford, which took her to Cameroon in West Africa. In 1982 she married Oliver Davies. They spent two years in Germany and then in 1985 came to live in Gwynedd. Fiona Bowie is a tutor in Women's Studies for the Open University in Wales and works as a freelance writer and part-time lecturer at University College North Wales, Bangor.

M. A. K. Duggan practices Medicine.

Judith Maro was born in Jerusalem in 1927. She read Law and Oriental Studies at Jerusalem University and has worked as a writer, journalist, translator and book reviewer. Her publications include *Atgofion Haganah* (memoir), *Y Porth nid â'n Angof* (novel), *Hen Wlad Newydd* (essays), *The Remembered Gate* (novel) and *Y Carlwm* (novel).

George Askey was born in Rhymney, Gwent. He has had a distinguished career in education in Wales and England, and is currently Deputy Director of Education in Mid Glamorgan.

Neil Edward Caldwell was born in London in 1952. He studied in Aberystwyth, and became Chairman of the National Union of Students, Wales. He is presently Director of the Council for the Protection of Rural Wales.

Joseph Clancy was born in 1928 in New York City, and holds his Ph.D. from Fordham University. He recently retired as Professor of English at Marymount Manhattan College, where he taught for over forty years. He and his wife are presently living in Aberystwyth. In addition to his selected poems, *The Significance of Flesh* (1984), Dr Clancy has produced seven books of translations from medieval and modern Welsh literature, including *The Plays of Saunders Lewis*, *Selected Poems by Bobi Jones* and a forthcoming collection of Kate Roberts's short stories. He was elected to the English Language Section of The Welsh Academy in 1971.

Tony Bianchi was born in North Shields in 1952. He studied in Lampeter, and became a lecturer and Fellow of the University of Wales. He is presently Literature Director of the Welsh Arts Council, and has numerous publications on Anglo-Welsh writers.

Greg Hill was born in London in 1949. He is a graduate of University College of Wales, Aberystwyth, where he also did research on the writer and painter David Jones. He was Reviews Editor and subsequently Editor of the *Anglo-Welsh Review* from 1979 to 1988. He is a frequent contributor to literary journals and has published a monograph on Llewelyn Wyn Griffith in the Writers in Wales series. He is currently lecturing at Coleg Ceredigion, Aberystwyth.